THE BOOK

of

SNUFF AND SNUFF BOXES

FIG. 1. LARGE COMMUNAL OR GUILD MULL
Fine Rams Horn. Mounted in Silver. Close of 18th century.

THE BOOK OF

Snuff and Snuff Boxes

BY

MATTOON M. CURTIS

*Formerly Professor of Philosophy, Western
Reserve University, and Member Royal
Society of Arts, London*

WITH 119 RARE AND UNUSUAL REPRODUCTIONS OF
SNUFF BOXES IN VARICOLORED GOLD, SILVER, IVORY,
AND PRECIOUS WOODS AND STONES

LIVERIGHT PUBLISHING CORPORATION

New York

MANUFACTURED IN THE UNITED STATES OF AMERICA
BY THE VAN REES PRESS

TABLE OF CONTENTS

PART ONE

TEXT

INTRODUCTION

THIS little book is the offspring of a desire
to make clear to myself the rise, development
and disappearance of the great vogue of snuffing
tobacco which for about three hundred years
played one of the most dramatic rôles in the
social life of modern peoples. Tobacco, pipes,
and smoking have their several histories, but
one looks in vain for the story of snuff, or
snuffers or snuff containers. I am not aware of
any monograph in this field although the wide
literature of tobacco furnishes many vagrant yet
interesting references to each aspect of our subject. This neglect of systematic or historical
treatment is surprising in view of the fact that
for about one hundred years historians have
been claiming a representation of the habits,
customs, fashions, and social aspects of organised societies. Yet to-day one must revert, even
in the English language, about one hundred
years to Fairholt, Billings, and Bragge to get a
reliable history of tobacco and its various forms

of consumption. Equally surprising is this neglect from an æsthetic point of view when we realise the undoubted facts that the snuff boxes of Europe and the snuff bottles of China constitute one of the most complete popular expressions, if not the most complete expression of occidental and oriental art for about two hundred years. The scholastic world has fallen upon evil days when it adopts commercial standards, "sells education," pushes its elective curriculum into the form of an up-to-date department store or cafeteria and repudiates unity, continuity, and totality by producing those expert or specialised crazy quilts of syndicated history, syndicated science, and syndicated philosophy where overlappings, contradictions, and lacunae are the consternation of the student. It is to be hoped that these murderous assaults upon literature, art, and education will pass with the present obsession of radical empiricism and pluralism.

Our brief story of the rise, extension and disappearance of snuffing, as well as our reflections on historical vagaries, make no claim to completeness or to exemption from error in this interesting and dramatic episode. Quite enough heresy in the field of current orthodoxy is present in the following pages to invite criticism and further study. The strange persistence of traditional error justifies our special effort to relegate the Nicot, Raleigh and Rook myths from the serious history of tobacco to the field of fiction or romance.

It is a curious fact in the realm of fashion that in both occident and orient the cessation of ostensible snuffing was synchronous—about the middle of the nineteenth century. From this time the picturesque snuff boxes, bottles and mulls became more desirable to collectors and to museums; and more inviting to fraudulent commercialism. It was during the debacle of the fine arts that Thackeray wrote in his *Paris Sketch Book*, 1840, "The Palace of Versailles has been turned into a bric-a-brac shop of late years, and its time-honoured walls have been covered with many thousand yards of the worst pictures that eye ever looked on." The æsthetic poverty of America in domestic snuff containers throughout the vogue of snuffing was due mainly to the economic pressure of colonisation, of wars, of pioneering, and to puritanic and democratic adherence to the simplicities of life.

The illustrations are intended to give some

idea of the great variety of materials, forms and decorations presented by snuff containers. If we should take current commercial art and museum exhibitions as a standard of taste our talk would be gratuitous for the ornate snuff box would be as much out of place to-day as a bobbed hair and skull-capped female would be in a miniature. The present vogue of no pictures on the walls of the home is not a compliment to contemporary art, while the extensive reproductions of old-time furniture are reminders that the sense of beauty and elegance has not vanished. This reflection encourages us to believe that a few illustrations of the monarchic, and aristocratic, and democratic types of snuff containers will not be unwelcome. As regards time, place, and relations of individual pieces our reticence is in sharp contrast with the volubility of the dealer, and we hesitate to say, "it is said." Even costume is not a valid criterion, as was shown long ago by Dürer. We are accustomed to think of France as the superlative in art without reflecting that she has never produced a painter or a musician of the first magnitude. France has furnished more snuff boxes of a high order than any other country, yet

she probably has no miniaturist superior to the
English Cosway and no market values that rival
two or three German boxes. We have avoided
footnotes which are a disturbing factor to the
ordinary reader by giving the impression that
he is missing something if he does not read them
and the contrary conviction if he does. As a
substitute our final chapter gives a select bibliography, with some comments, which will an-
swer all demands of the critical reader and at
the same time give a general view of our many
obligations. If this survey throws a ray of light
upon the perturbations of our common human
nature, and gives some assistance in pursuing a
delightful journey into this particular field of
the beautiful, its purposes will be realised.

M.M.C.

CHAPTER I

Tobacco in Aboriginal America

A SURVEY of the habits of primitive people, especially as they advance in culture, justifies the statement that man has universally drunk, smoked, chewed, and snuffed something not necessarily connected with his normal diet. Various plants—roots, barks, leaves, blossoms, and fruits—have been used for these purposes. All the ancient medicine men or physicians, including Hippocrates, prescribed for human ills the drinking of the juices, or the inhaling of the smoke or dust, or the chewing of the roots, barks, and leaves of certain plants. The smoke of hempseed was used by the ancient Scythians, Thracians, and Babylonians for both medicinal and narcotic effects, opium serving the same purpose in the Far East. It is only within the last hundred years that the *materia medica* has much changed.

[15]

American peoples Stahl has corrected a common error by showing that pipes in various
forms and materials were widely used by the
aborigines even in Ecuador and Peru.

Why the tobacco plant was first domesticated
by the Indians we do not know. Its æsthetic
appeal may have been a factor, but its effects
on the human organism are far more probable.
In any case it is *Waka*, the mysterious and valuable gift of the Great Spirit to his children.
Nor do we know when its uses arose. From an
archæological point of view the relatively in-
destructible pipe takes us back at least two
thousand years, and this is probably a brief
period in the many uses of tobacco by the early
Americans. One might suppose no prehistoric
evidence of the perishable snuff, cigar, or cigarette, yet the old shrine-caves of Arizona have
yielded thousands of cigarettes, votive offerings
made long before the discovery of the New
World. Thus we may hold a permanent possibility of new discoveries in the prehistory of
tobacco. Allowing for sectional variations and
emphases we may enumerate the uses of tobacco among the aborigines as follows: (1) A
curative of certain diseases, sores, wounds, and

a defence against insects and pests; (2) A preventive of hunger, thirst, and fatigue; a restorative of physical and mental energy; (3) a factor in all religious, civil and social ceremonies, tobacco being considered the best gift to man and to visiting chiefs in council, and being often used at birth, marriage, and funeral ceremonies; (4) a source of pleasure to taste and smell, and effective at the same time as a narcotic and a stimulant in different modes of consumption; (5) a medium of exchange or barter—a sort of wampum. We must not generalise all or any one of these uses, for possibly Prescott correctly remarks, "The Peruvians differed from any other nation to whom tobacco was known by using it only for medicinal purposes in the form of snuff."

The early explorers were looking for gold, and the fringes of their observation were very contracted. Even Columbus on his first landing at San Salvador, October 12, 1492, when presented with golden tobacco leaves threw them away not knowing they were the most precious gifts the Indians could bring—far more precious to these "benighted savages" than the gold which civilised Europe craved, and for the possession of which she was ready to resort to treachery, rapine and murder. Still, they did note that the natives everywhere were using tobacco, and as early as 1503 the Spaniards found that the Indian device of bloodless warfare was to squirt tobacco juice into the eyes of the enemy. This accomplishment had its counterpart later in the American cowboy who could say to the tenderfoot, "Sit still, stranger, I'll clear you," and hit the cuspidor twenty feet away. Chewing seems to have been a common practice, especially when hard work or long marches were demanded. It has been said that an Indian could trek for two or three days with no other support against hunger, thirst, and fatigue than tobacco. It was an interesting custom of several American tribes to mix lime or finely powdered burned shells with their chewing tobacco, for this is precisely what was done by the Andean highlanders who chewed the coco leaf and by the betel-nut chewers in the East Indies. Tobacco was a part of the medicine man's kit and he used it not only to put himself in revery or dream or ecstasy for prophecy, but as a cure of wounds and diseases, for colds, headache, and vascular difficulties. No wonder that the American aborigines generally regarded the tobacco plant as their most valuable possession, and that it was regarded as a gift of the Great Spirit!

To assert the religious origin of the uses of tobacco is fanciful or meaningless. Shall we infer that the eating of bread and the drinking of wine had a religious origin because they were thus used in the agape? Among the most primitive as well as the most civilised, "Every good and perfect gift" is referred to God as the giver. Like all primitive people who has passed through savagery and barbarism, whatever these terms may mean, to the like vagueness of civilisation, the Mexicans and Peruvians believed their advancement and all elements of culture to be indigenous and the gifts of God. It was Pachacamac who created the Peruvian tribes with all their distinctions out of the one clay of the Titicaca valley. So with the Mexicans it was Quetzalcohuatl who communicated to them all the arts of life and the uses of the vegetable world. Only in this comprehensive sense may we speak of the religious origin of tobacco and its uses. The Indians sacrificed tobacco to God because it was the most valued thing they possessed in their daily lives. This is the meaning of sacrifice from the earliest Egyptian times to the offering by Abraham and the bringing of gold, frankincense, and myrrh to Bethlehem; this is the meaning of the smoking priests among the Mayas and Aztecs as pictured upon the tablets of Palenque; and this, too, was the meaning in that extraordinary culture represented by Montezuma, where the last duty of the youth chosen for sacrifice was to smoke a pipe of tobacco to the glory of God and the happiness of mankind.

On his second voyage Columbus was accompanied by a Spanish monk, Ramón Pane, who remained in San Domingo to study the customs of its people. In 1497 Pane wrote his *De Insularium Ritibus*, in which he says: "Snuffing is through a tube, one end placed over the powdered leaf and the other in the nose, and so drawn up, which purges them very much." This internal *lomi-lomi* plainly refers to the medicinal aspect of snuffing. Oviedo in his *Historia de las Indias*, 1526, speaks of snuffing tobacco smoke through the nostrils by means of a forked tube about a span long, and Bragge describes a similar device used by the Madeira

Indians of Brazil for taking dry snuff. As the snuffing of the smoke of tobacco rather than its powder is the only form of tobacco consumption not adopted by Europeans, this unique West Indian custom may be described briefly in the words of Oviedo, who is speaking directly of the Indians of San Domingo or Hispaniola. "They take it in this manner; the caciques or chief men have small hollow sticks a few inches long and of the thickness of the little finger. These pipes have two channels that merge into one, the whole being in one piece. The double end they set in the openings of the nostrils, the other end in the smoke of the burning herb. These pipes be right smoothe and well wrought. They inhale the smoke one, two and three times, and as often more as they can, until they fall senseless and lie for long upon the earth, unconscious, drunk and wrapped in profound slumber. The Indians who can not procure these little sticks take the smoke through common reeds or grasses. The instruments through which they inhale the smoke, the Indians call *tabaco*, but they do not (as some have thought) so name either the herb or the stupor that overcomes them. This herb the Indians regard as a very precious thing, and they grow it in their gardens and plantations for the purpose aforesaid." The few snuffing tubes which have been discovered and are now reposing in museums may be classified as the straight one-nostril tube; the straight two-nostril tubes bound together; the bifurcated Y tube about a span long; the X tube by which two persons blow snuff into each other's nostrils, and a triangular or V-shaped tube in which a pinch of snuff is put, then with one prong in the mouth and the other in the nostril an exhaling puff shoots the snuff into the nose. Surely the evolution of snuffing has not been from the simple to the complex but rather like all machinery quite the reverse. Not even a Scotchman with all the paraphernalia of the mull could vie with these aristocrats of Peru, Brazil and the West Indies in their snuff making and snuff taking. They must have entered fully into the joys of invention and of the superfluous. Cortes found tobacco widely cultivated in Mexico, and also that the Mexicans were acquainted with it as a powder to be snuffed by the nose in order to produce sneezing thus relieving colds and stoppages in the head, while he found that at the court of Montezuma tobacco for smoking and snuffing was scented with various gums and roses. We are informed by the early Portuguese explorers that the Indians of Brazil had snuff mills, and that their product was "the finest in the world." Billings quotes Ewbank as saying: "Columbus first beheld smokers in the Antilles, Pizarro found chewers in Peru, but it was in the country discovered by Cabral that the great sternutatory was originally found. Brazilian Indians were the fathers of snuff and its best fabricators." One of their methods was to make a cup in a rosewood block and with a pestle of the same wood pulverise the leaves of tobacco into the finest powder, this friction giving the most delicate rosewood aroma to the hot snuff. The snuff, still hot, was put into bone tubes the ends of which were plugged to preserve the rich fragrance. These mills and snuff tubes were finely decorated, and could be easily carried from place to place. It is quite probable that the quality of this product has never been surpassed. Alexander von Humboldt describes quite a different snuff made by the Otomacs, who gathered the long pods of a mimosa, cut them in pieces, moistened them and caused them to ferment, mixed with the

[25]

flour of cassava and lime procured from the shell of a helix. The whole mass was exposed to a brisk fire. When it was to be used it was reduced to a very fine powder and placed in a dish. The snuffer held the dish in the right hand and inhaled the *niopo* by the nose, through the forked bone of a bird. Father Gumilla says, "This diabolical powder of the Otomacs, furnished by an arborescent tobacco plant, intoxicates them by the nostrils, deprives them of reason, and renders them furious in battle." Niopo, widely used as snuff, was not *tabacum* though similar in smell and effects.

This method stands in sharp contrast to the general manner of the North American Indians in preparing the tobacco leaf for use. The leaves were sun- or fire- or wigwam-cured, then rubbed in the hands or put into a mortar to be pulverised. Often the whole leaf, sometimes the soft parts only, and again the stems alone were mortared. As a rule the finest powder was used for snuff and the coarser parts for smoking and chewing. Even the forerunners of the later snuff-, cigar-, and cigarette-box are found among the American aborigines—animal bones and gourds for the storage of snuff, and bark boxes and skin pouches for the storage of rolls of tobacco in various sized leaves, and for mortar products. Nor did the Indians lack fastidiousness of taste in the mixtures of tobacco with other plants, such as red willow, partridge, yew, and sumac, and in flavouring their mixtures with various barks, musks, and gums. Some of the Indians prepared their chewing tobacco with powdered shells, which might suggest a plug or twist or carotte or moist snuff.

The discussion of the origin of the name "tobacco" is fruitless. Among the many tribes of natives different names are given to the plant. In Brazil *petum* or *petun* was the most general, and it was adopted by the Portuguese. In the great Caribbean district there are several places named Tobaco, or Tobago, any one of which might satisfy patronymic curiosity. But some writers are of the opinion that as the Y-shaped tube by which the powder and smoke of the weed was snuffed was called tobacco, by metonymy it became the name of the weed. Uhle believes "there is no doubt that the modern name of tobacco is derived from the word *taboca* of Tupi origin which in Haiti signified tube." Nor can we be sure just how far the Spaniards and Portuguese in the early days stimulated the production of tobacco. We know they were very friendly to the development, that their sailors were known as "incorrigible smokers," that they introduced slave labour to the West Indies, and soon began the exportation of tobacco to Europe.

It was one hundred and twenty years after the discovery of tobacco that the English colonists at Jamestown, Virginia, began its cultivation. Seven years later, 1619, a Dutch man-of-war sold twenty negroes to these planters. In 1620 the production for the English market was about 60,000 pounds, and the price of an imported young white woman was 120 pounds of tobacco. But the thraldom of the white man to tobacco began in Cuba, Tuesday, November 6, 1492, when his interpreters of oriental languages, Rodrigo de Jerez and Luis de Torres, after a five days' visit to the interior, reported to Columbus that they saw many natives "puffing smoke from their mouths and noses." Tobacco's first speedy conquest was the maritime world, then the great port cities, and finally the Church and State capitals of the

world.   About 1575 it was used in every nation
of the earth including Japan and the Philippine
Islands.   The immediate social effects of the
discovery of tobacco are suggested in these lines,
which might have been written in Spanish or
Portuguese at least sixty years before the time
of Hawkins:

Up comes brave Hawkins on the beach—
   "Shiver my hull!" he cries;
"What's these here games, my merry men?"
   And then, "Why blame my eyes!
Here's one as chaws, and one as snuffs,
   And t'other of the three
Is smoking like a chimney-pot —
   They've found out Tobac-kee!"

CHAPTER II

THE INTRODUCTION OF TOBACCO
TO EUROPE

THE discovery of America aroused Europe
and drew attention to the men and things of a
new world. Many expeditions went forth from
Lisbon, Cadiz, and the Mediterranean ports of
France and Italy. Holland and England soon
followed in the exploitation of new lands and
seas. The returning Spanish and Portuguese
sailors were the first to acquaint their people
with tobacco and its uses. Las Casas, the greatest missionary of the old world to the new, in
his preservation of the journals of Columbus,
fully justifies Singer in saying: "There can be
no doubt that the knowledge of tobacco reached
the old world from America, and that the first
acquaintance of Europeans with the herb is
contemporary, almost to a day, with the discovery of the western continent." Columbus
himself records at least three instances where
[30]

tobacco and its uses were called to his attention. Rodrigo de Jerez, who was with Columbus on his first voyage, and was the first European to set foot on Cuban soil, was also the first man to be arrested and imprisoned for smoking by the Inquisition. Had he remained in port he would have been safe, but when his fellow-townsmen of Ayamonte saw smoke pouring from his mouth and nose they regarded him as a minion of the Devil. Thus technically the smoking of tobacco was introduced to Europe soon after the return of Columbus, and we infer from the analogies of nautical experience that the chewing and snuffing of tobacco were not long strangers in southern European ports.

Early in the sixteenth century, physicians, especially in Seville and Salamanca, and professors in some of the universities became interested in the curative powers of tobacco. In 1523 Giovanni Verazzano, in a letter to Francis I of France, called attention to the medicinal properties of tobacco and its smoke. It is not our present purpose either to present or discuss the extravagant medical claims for tobacco in the sixteenth century. This extravagance is rivalled by the social claims for tobacco in 1924 by Laufer who writes: "The association of coffee with tobacco is very close, and their alliance has stimulated and promoted thought, scholarship, literature and art; it probably affected social customs, intensified sociability, and paved the way to the era of humanism. Of all the gifts of nature, tobacco has been the most potent social factor, the most efficient peacemaker, and a great benefactor to mankind. It has made the whole world akin, and united it into a common bond. Of all luxuries it is the most democratic and the most universal; it has contributed a large share toward democratising the world." One might infer from this either that sociology in the twentieth century has arrived at about the position of medicine in the sixteenth century, or that the long-despised philosophy of history is finally in the saddle.

When we raise the question as to the domestication of the tobacco plant and its wider use in Europe we are in trouble with contradictions, anachronisms, and myths. History may repeat itself with variations, but historians repeat historians with dull monotony. It is perhaps well to remember that until recently history was elliptical, having as its two centres church and

state. Whatever did not float into these two
realms was negligible or did not exist. To exist
tobacco had to arrive at court, or become the
concern of the state, or come under the purview
of the church, as in the case of Rodrigo. One
of the complaints of James I against tobacco
was that "it was neither broght in by King, great
Conqueror, nor learned Doctor of Phisike."
Without discussion we accept the view that the
tobacco plant was domesticated in Spain and
Portugal about 1519—Nadaillac says 1518.
Singer, who has made a special study of this
period, says it is not unlikely that the first introduction of the plant into Europe was by Her-
nando Cortés, the conqueror of Mexico, who
is said to have presented tobacco seeds to Charles
V in 1518. In France and Holland production
began not much later than 1550. Corti says,
"Tobacco was widely cultivated in Holland as
early as 1560, partly owing to the presence of
refugees from religious persecutions in France."
This rapid development was due largely to the
growing belief in the prophylactic and curative
effects of tobacco, but apart from this it had
opened up new avenues of delight in the mysterious regions of taste and smell.

[33]

In 1559 Henry II of France sent his private
secretary, Jean Nicot, 1530-1600, as ambassador to Lisbon to bring about the marriage of his
daughter to Sebastian, the King of Portugal.
This mission failed, and Nicot turned his attention to tobacco, which he discovered growing
in the gardens of Lisbon. Here we must fol-
low Frampton, who in his English translation
of Monardes, 1577, introduced a special chapter not in Monardes, captioned "Nicotiana,"
the content of which apparently he had received
from his friend Nicot. But appearances are
here deceptive, as a casual reading of Frampton's "Nicotiana" chapter suggests that its author is a Frenchman, France being the country
referred to as "This Realme." As Frampton
gives no hint that he is not the author and offers
no other source of information than Nicot we
turn to the Tudor edition of Frampton's Monardes, 1925, with an introduction by Stephen
Gaselee covering twenty-seven pages, and find
no ray of light on any question. The facts are
that the "Nicotiana" chapter has no background
in Monardes; that it is a close translation by
Frampton of *L'agriculture et la maison rustique,* book II, chapter 76 of the sixth edition,

Paris 1570; that this edition had not a dual authorship as generally asserted but was essentially the work of Jean Liebault, the son-in-law of Charles Estienne; that Jean Liebault received directly from Nicot the "Nicotiana" chapter, thus accounting for the use of first personal pronouns in the Liebault chapter. Why Frampton did not acquaint his readers with this important information does not concern us here. We turn now to Nicot's appraisal of himself in the Liebault "Nicotiana" chapter. Liebault concludes this chapter with the words: "Lo, here have you the true Historie of Nicotiane of the whiche the saide Lorde Nicot, one of the Kinge's Counsellors, first founder out of this hearbe, hath made me privee as well by woorde as by writyng." Nicot represented himself to his credulous friend Liebault as "the finder out by careful experimentation of the wonderful medicinal and curative properties of tobacco for severe cuts and bruises, as well as for Noli-me-tangere, all old Soares, and cankered Ulcers, hurtes, Ringwormes, greate scabbes, dropsie, short breathes, Kinge's evill * * * * and the people began to name it the Ambassador's hearbe, * * * the first authour, in-

[35]

venter, and bringer of this hearbe into France. * * * and (the one who) did send it to King Fraunces the Seconde, and to the Queen Mother, and to many other Lordes of the Courte, with the manner of governyng the same; and how to applie it unto saide diseases, even as he had found it by experience." Finally, the origin of the word is given: "This Hearbe is called Nicotiane, of the name of hym that gave the firste intelligence thereof into this Realme * * * for that he hath in-riched our Countrie, with so singular an hearbe."

Nicot's story reminds me of an incident during a voyage, when a friend said to me, "Do you know we have on board the greatest photographer in the world?" I replied, "I will take your word for it." He retorted, "Don't do that—he told me so himself." Without giving Talleyrand's definition of diplomacy, we may note that seven years before Nicot was born the attention of Francis I of France was called to the medical properties of tobacco, and that Diego Columbus, the eldest son of Christopher, in his will dated May 2nd, 1523, made a legacy to a tobacco merchant in Lisbon. About 1541,

Girolamo Benzoni of Milan, in writing his
History of the New World, records his disgust
of the "sharp fetid smell" of tobacco, and ex-
claims, "See what a wicked and pestiferous
poison from the devil this must be." Yet he
notes that the American medicine men treated
the sick by administering tobacco smoke and
"when the patient was thoroughly intoxicated
by it the cure was mostly effected." Still relating his experiences in America Benzoni gives a
list of the curative powers of tobacco, saying:
"These leaves are strung together, hung in the
shade and dried, and used whole or powdered,
and are considered good for headaches, lock-
jaw, toothache, coughs, asthma, stomach-ache,
obstructions, kidney troubles, diseases of the
heart, rheumatism, the poisoning from arrows,
carbuncles, polypus, consumption." In 1535
the great French explorer Jacques Cartier in his
second exploration of the St. Lawrence River
describes the uses of tobacco, *rustica*, among the
natives of that area. Thus about twenty years
before Nicot made his wonderful discoveries at
Lisbon the attention of Europe was being called
to tobacco and its uses by first-hand historians.
Another Frenchman closely connected with the

court, André Thevet, was growing tobacco at Angoulême in France several years before Nicot set out for Lisbon. Thevet introduced the best Brazilian *tabacum*, the plant which France clung to for her great revenues, while Nicot, according to his own story, introduced the inferior *rustica* from Florida without explaining how the Portuguese could have secured the *rustica* from Florida. Presuming a minimum of intelligence the French Court must have heard of tobacco long before it was discovered and announced by Nicot. Laufer expresses surprise that Thevet did not push his claims at court, but even supposing Thevet eager for priority what chance had he against "Lord Nicot," the *protégé* of Catherine and the prescriber of tobacco for the many ills and frequent headaches of the royal family. Laufer makes the astonishing claim that there were "two introductions," and "that France owes her tobacco to Thevet and Nicot equally." This is a doubly bad straddle when one considers *tabacum* and *rustica* as well as indubitable dates. Thus at the present moment we agree with Paul Gaffarel, "The legitimate vindication of Thevet has never found hearing." Nicot probably in-

[38]

troduced tobacco effectively to the court of France and on his return to Paris in 1561 recommended tobacco smoke or powder taken through the nostrils. With the single exception of Thevet's protest of Nicot's audacity (see Thevet) Nicot is the only one who, in the extension of tobacco to every nation of the earth, has ever made a claim either of invention, or of discovery, or of introduction. He claims all three. In 1570 the botanical name *Nicotiana* was given to tobacco by Nicot and Jean Liebault of Paris, in 1577 it captioned the chapter "Nicotiana" in Frampton's Monardes, and in the eighteenth century the name *Nicotine* was given to the active, toxic element by Linnæus. Thus Nicot, failing to marry Marguerite to Sebastian, succeeded diplomatically in marrying himself to tobacco forever.

But we must not ignore the Catherine de' Medici, 1519-89, widow of Henry II and mother of Charles IX, for about 1572 the scholars called tobacco *Herbe Médicée*, while it was more popularly known as *Herbe de la Reine*. Was Catherine the "Queen of Snuffers"? We do not know. Could Catherine live with tobacco for nearly forty years and not know all about it experimentally? We do not know. We have no indubitable proof. Still, "the argument from silence" would leave many a hero unborn, and most of the people who were born still alive. Perhaps Bishops Berkeley and Butler were right in holding that probability is the test of truth. Assuming that Catherine was as innocent of snuffing as of the events of St. Bartholomew's day we are at no loss for evidence that the practice of snuffing arose within the French court circle about 1560, and is thus *au règle*, as it could not have arisen elsewhere. Nicot's "Grande Prior of France," better known as the Duke of Lorraine, made the acquaintance of tobacco while visiting Nicot in Lisbon where tobacco, including snuff, was a merchandise. The Duke became an habitual snuff taker using three ounces daily and, according to Liebault, propagated snuffing in France more than any one else. Laufer is incorrect in saying that from this time in France "snuff remained the only mode of taking tobacco on the part of gentlemen until the nineteenth century." This ignores the fact that smoking took possession of the court under Henry IV and that Louis XIII and Richelieu had much trouble in changing the court habit to snuffing.

The introduction of tobacco to England has been variously attributed to Hawkins, Lane, Drake, and Raleigh. Recently Singer has written: "It was not until July 28, 1586, that Francis Drake, with Governor Lane and Walter Raleigh on board, brought to England the first tobacco that reached this country." On evidential ground we must dissent from this opinion, and while not able to fix any definite date we assume that tobacco was in England as early as the close of Hawkins's second voyage in 1565. Considering that this date is about twenty years after the introduction of tobacco to China, Japan, and the Philippines according to Conti, and considering also the intimate relations of England with Spain and Portugal, we are putting a sufficient strain upon "English insularity." Before referring to documentary proof of the correctness of our view, it is important to notice the Raleigh and the Rook traditions which are current even in the sober histories of our own day.

In song and story Sir Walter Raleigh, 1552-1618, holds the centre of the stage. We recall how this gallant courtier cast his mantle before the queen so that her majesty's feet might not touch the unhallowed moisture of English soil; how he introduced smoking into the court, and to Elizabeth, and demonstrated to her that tobacco smoke could be weighed; how his high social position and example made smoking popular throughout the realm, including the House of Lords; how in the Mermaid Tavern he inoculated Ben Jonson, Shakespeare, Beaumont, Fletcher, Selden, and possibly Bacon with what Jonson describes as "the most soothing, sovereign and precious weed that ever our dear old Mother Earth tendered to the use of man"; how following an Indian custom of inhaling or swallowing smoke he brought to England the continental nomenclature "drinking tobacco"; how working at his desk and at his pipe he was doused by a pail of water by a servant moved by impulse on a first impression or by reasoning that where there was so much smoke there must be some fire; how he was criticised for smoking at the execution of Essex, and later for smoking on his own journey to the scaffold. Such are some of the traditions associated with the most romantic and dramatic figure in English history and in the story of tobacco.

The glamour of the name Raleigh and its associations with tobacco should not blind us to the fact that Sir Walter never thought of himself as introducing tobacco and smoking to England. This was first done by his enemy King James, who in his *Counterblast* ignorantly assumed that the discovery of Virginia and the appearance of tobacco in England were contemporaneous, and who refers to smoking as a "vile barbarous custom brought in by a father so generally hated," the "father" being of course Raleigh. A few years later James took the opportunity to please both Spain and himself by executing Sir Walter. Public opinion as it was in England at this time is much better expressed in the lines written long after the death of James:

Sir Walter Raleigh! name of worth,
How sweet for thee to know,
King James who never smoked on earth,
Is smoking down below.

Before Raleigh left England on his first voyage to America, 1584, he might have equipped himself with a sufficient supply of tobacco from the London market, and at the same time purchased copies of Thevet's *The New Founde World* and of Frampton's Monardes at any important bookshop. Indeed the old tar with arm outstretched toward the sea, lecturing the boy Raleigh, so admirably painted by Millais, might well have had a bit of tobacco within his cheek.

As regards the beginning of snuffing tobacco in England we have the familiar story that in 1702 George Rooke captured near Cadiz "several thousand barrels of very choice Spanish snuff," which he took to England, where it was christened Vigo snuff and sold at very reasonable rates. Even Haydn's *Dictionary of Dates* says that "snuff taking took its rise in England" from this event. Billings quotes English statistics of the reign of Queen Anne to show that there were in London at this time, 1702, no less than seven thousand shops where snuff was sold. These Spanish and English snuff figures seem enormous, but as an explanation of the beginnings of snuff in England they are comic. Count Corti in his interesting *History of Smoking* holds that "snuff was introduced into England by the courtiers and officers who had been with Charles II in France," about 1660. (This is as surprising as his statement that syphilis was introduced to Europe from America. Even bibliography shows that the former is Elizabethan and the latter of the Roman Empire. Sailors brought the former to Europe and the latter to America and Polynesia.) Butler in his *Hudibras* tells us that the saints of the Cromwellian period were not averse to snuff. Although Cromwell ordered his cavalry to trample down the tobacco fields of England he enjoyed the pipe and possibly the snuff box. In a popular satire of the time, *News from the New Exchange*, 1650, the Puritan Mistress Campbell held the socially significant maxim:

"She that with pure tobacco will not prime
Her nose, can be no lady of the time."

If this was the situation among the purists and Roundheads many years before Corti's date for the introduction of snuff into England, what must have been the habits of the Tories, Cavaliers, Anglicans, and other people of "the world, the flesh and the devil"? In the polite literature

[45]

from 1600 to 1650 there are many references to snuff, ladles, and boxes. Even in the sixteenth century Henry Buttes, 1599, speaks of a tobacco "which the nose sooneth taketh in snuffe." Dekker, picturing the manners of his time in *The Gulls Hornbook*, 1602, speaks of "the ladle for the cold snuff into the nostril," and though the instruments for snuff making are seldom dated, Bragge describes a boxwood cylindrical snuff mill with three belts of carved figures dated 1607. If we could conjure up Ben Jonson, who carried snuff loose in his pocket, he would probably have something interesting to say as to when snuff first appeared in England.

There is ample documentary evidence to show that tobacco was introduced, cultivated and widely used in England long before the days of Raleigh's voyage to America. One of his companions gives us the first account of Virginia tobacco, then *rustica* but much later *tabacum*. In Thomas Harriot's *A brief and true report of the new found land of Virginia*, 1588, we read: "There is an herbe which is sowed a part by itselfe & is called by the inhabitants *vppówoc:* In the West Indies it hath diuers

names, according to the seuerall places & countries where it groweth and is vsed: The Span-
iardes generally called it *Tobacco*. The leaues
thereof being dried and brought into powder:
they vse to take the fume of smoke thereof by
sucking it through pipes made of claie into their
stomacke and heade; from whence it purgeth
superfluous fleame & other grosse humors, open-
eth all the pores & passages of the body: by
which meanes the vse thereof, not only preseru-
eth the body from obstructions; but also if any
be, so that they haue not beene of too long con-
tinuance, in short time it breaketh them:
whereby their bodies are notably preserued in
health, & know not many greeuous diseases
wherewithall wee in England are oftentimes
afflicted. This Vppówoc is of so precious esti-
mation amongest thē, that they thinke their
gods are maruelously delighted therwith:
Wherupon sometime they make hallowed fires
& cast some of the pouder therein for a sacrifice:
being in a storme vppon the waters, to pacifie
their gods, they cast some vp into the aire and
into the water: so a weare for fish being newly
set vp, they cast some therein and into the aire:
also after an escape of danger, they cast some

[47]

into the aire likewise: but all done with strange gestures, stamping, sometime dauncing, clapping of hands, holding vp of hands, & staring vp into the heaues, vttering therewithal & chattering strange words & noises. We our selues during the time we were there vsed to suck it after their maner, as also since our returne, & haue found manie rare and wonderful experiments of the vertues thereof; of which the relation woulde require a volume by itselfe: the vse of it by so manie of late, men & women of great calling as else, and some learned Phisitions also, is sufficient witnes." The prevalence of smoking in England is also witnessed by a German traveller, Paul Heutzner who in his *Itinerarium*, or Journey to England, 1598, says: "At bull-baiting, bear-whipping, and everywhere else the English are constantly smoking the Nicotian weed, which in America is called 'Tobaco.'" Singer has noted that, at this time, 1598, a handbook for seamen was published and dedicated to Queen Elizabeth, recommending tobacco juice for erysipelas and skin lesions, and that this remedy was probably used until recent times.

Partington, in his *Smoke Rings and Roun-*

delays, notes that "in the State Archives there is still extant an edict issued by Queen Elizabeth against the use and abuse of tobacco, dated 1584 —the year Raleigh's first expedition sailed to the new world." The early use of tobacco in England is further emphasised by L'Obel's work on botany, 1570, which records that "the West Indian tobacco plant has become an inmate of England." Harrison's *Chronicle* or *Great Chronologie* shows that tobacco was smoked in England as early as 1573: "In these daies the taking-in of the smoke of the Indian herbe called Tabaco, by an instrument formed like a little ladell, whereby it passeth from the mouth into the hed and stomach, is greatlie taken up and used in England." MacInnes holds that "Tobacco probably reached England during the reign of Queen Mary as a result of the close connection which at that time existed between England and Spain." Both Taylor the Water Poet and Edmund Howes of Stow's *Annals* say that tobacco was first brought into England by Hawkins, who returned from his second voyage September 20, 1565. This view is confirmed by John Sparkes, the younger, who in his account of this voyage shows that

Hawkins became acquainted with tobacco in Florida. In view of these evidences and of the estimate by Barnaby Rich in his *Honestie of this Age*, 1614, that the tobacco trade of London was 319,275 pounds sterling, quite apart from the enormous activity in smuggling, we may conclude that at about this time,

> *"Prince and peasant, lord and lackey,*
> *All in some form take their Baccy."*

It is one of the comedies of human life that Europe rioted in American tobacco for more than one hundred and twenty-five years before she recognised the value of the American potato, which according to Alexander von Humboldt and Goethe was as great a blessing as tobacco was a curse. The imperious fascination of tobacco throughout Europe is suggested by the Scotchman who when told by his physician that if he continued smoking he would soon be blind, replied after a moment's reflection, "Weel, I am athinking I h'ae seen about everything."

CHAPTER III

European Opposition to Tobacco

When the Inquisition arrested and imprisoned Rodrigo for smoking it did not take any definite position as regards tobacco in general but only against the alarming phenomena of this form of its consumption. That this alarm quickly subsided is evident, for on Rodrigo's release after a few years he found some of his fellows smoking without fear of imprisonment. It is interesting to note that from these days of Columbus to the present the great tobacco controversy has been almost wholly concerned with smoking. Some recent scientific reports on tobacco and health do not even mention chewing and snuffing, although the production for these exercises is enormous.

From the beginning, smoking has often been a private and a public nuisance. It has always kept the forest fires, as well as the home fires, burning. In the early days of steel, flint, tinder and coals, complaints of property damage were common. Nothing can be more disgusting than a room after a smoking bee, or the halitosis caused by a foul pipe or a bad cigar. Still for about one hundred years after its discovery there was little opposition to tobacco, partly because it was largely confined to port towns, and was often dispensed in cities by pharmacists only. The chief reason for the delay of organised opposition was the reputation of tobacco as a cure-all, supported by many leading physicians in all parts of Europe. In 1576 L'Obel, one of the leading botanists of his time, says of tobacco, "it satisfieth hunger, it helps ulcers and wounds, and it is good for diseases of the chest and the wasting of the lungs. In fact there is no new thing that our age has obtained from America that is more efficacious as a remedy." Chewing, smoking, snuffing, fresh tobacco leaves, and various tobacco ointments were specific centres for as many groups of diseases, and the general attitude toward tobacco might be expressed then as now:

> *For rich and poor, in peace or strife,*
> *It smooths the rugged path of life.*

To Spenser in his *Faerie Queene*, 1590, it is "divine tobacco"; in Ben Jonson's *"Every Man in his Humour,"* 1596, Bobadilla says, " 'tis most divine"; to Lilly, court poet to Elizabeth, 1597, tobacco is "our holy herbe nicotian"; in John Davies, 1598, it is "an herb of heavenly power."

But by 1600 the times were ripening for an onslaught against the rapidly rising use of tobacco throughout Europe. There was a growing scepticism regarding its medicinal values. There was a well-founded suspicion that the axiom, "prevention is better than cure" was leading people to anticipate all the diseases for which tobacco was a remedy. Pharmacology had succumbed to prophylaxis. Under puritanic influences it was coming to be regarded as a wicked comfort and luxury. Church and state saw in its popularity an extravagant expenditure of money that should go elsewhere, and especially a corrupting element in their official families. Antagonism began to show itself in the press and on the bema by those who loved negation or sought reform.

A generous volume would be required to give even a brief survey of the pro and contra literature in this field. While some find in tobacco the cure of all the ills of life, others regard it as the cause of all human miseries. The latter have expanded the vocabulary of vituperation in every European language. We shall not dwell on the gruesome bloody persecutions of the users of tobacco in Russia, Turkey, Persia and elsewhere; nor the cutting off of the heads, the noses and the tongues so intimately involved in smoking, chewing, and snuffing. A single example of this helpless and hopeless bigotry must suffice. In 1634 the Czar of Russia, Michael, decreed that for the first offence smokers should be whipped, and for the second offence executed, while snuff takers were to have the nose amputated. In a few words fit to print we may give the general drift of verbal opposition. Here is Joshua Sylvester, 1615, court poet to James I, who calls tobacco a "hell-dust, England's shame, a madness, a frenzy, that by the Devil's agency has been brought from the savages to England." Here is Robert Burton, 1620, who gives a melancholy view of it as "a plague, a mischief, a violent purger of goods, lands, health; hellish, devilish and damned tobacco, the ruin and overthrow of body and soul." Fairholt says, "Grave doctors were not wanting to declare that the brains of snuff takers were found after death, dried to a sort of dirty membrane, clogged with soot." Dr. John Hill, 1761, avers regarding snuff that "many persons have perished miserably of diseases occasioned or rendered incurable by its use." This Dr. Hill, later Sir John, was also a writer of farces. To him Garrick paid the epigrammatic compliment:

"For physic and farces his equal there scarce is;
His farces are physic, his physic a farce is."

Another poet, whose language is even less ornate than that of his Jacobean brother, represents the nineteenth century. Mr. Swinburne, the author of *Songs Before Sunrise*, remarks: "James I was a knave, a tyrant, a fool, a liar, a coward. But I love him, I worship him, because he slit the throat of the blackguard Raleigh who invented this filthy smoking." The cogency of such arguments has been ignored by an irrational world. An ample if mild summary lies in the familiar lines:

[55]

"Tobacco is an Indian weed,
From the devil it doth proceed,
It picks your pockets, burns your clothes,
And makes a chimney of your nose."

In this connection snuff might qualify as a chimney-sweep. Whether tobacco is to be referred to God or to the Devil is still an open question depending on the referee. A neglected argument against the use of manufactured tobacco is suggested by Fairholt in his remarks on Prescott's *Tobacco and Its Adulterations.* Among such adulterations the following substances have been used: leaves of rhubarb, dock, burdock, coltsfoot, beech, plantain, oak, elm, cabbage, lettuce and chicory leaves steeped in tar-oil. Other adulterations mentioned are peat-earth, bran, sawdust, malt-rootlets, barley-meal, pea-meal, and potato-starch. This brief list could easily be extended. Fairholt mentions a case in which a cigar manufacturer resisted successfully an attempt at enforcing the legal penalty for the unlawful fabrication of cheap "Havannah Cigars" from tobacco which had paid no duty, as he was able to show in his own defence that he never made use of the tobacco leaf at all.

We turn to a brief notice of church and state in this controversy. Elizabeth died in 1603, and James I, the devotee of absolutism and the divine right of kings, came to the throne of England. James had already sworn to himself to stamp out this "damnable tobacco," and he had all the foolhardiness of bigotry to aid him. The story is a long and fruitless one. To him Presbyterianism and tobacco were inventions of the Devil, while tobacco alone was "the lively image and pattern of hell." He prohibited tobacco-growing in England, and told the Virginians to quit raising tobacco and turn to mulberry trees and silkworms. He urged Parliament to raise duties on tobacco from two pence to six shillings and ten pence per pound. At this point we must correct some current historical errors. Laufer tells us that the import duty on tobacco was "raised by James in 1604 to 6s. 10d. per pound, (equal to 25s, present value), an advance of 4000 per cent. This heavy tax nearly ruined Virginia whose economic life was based on the cultivation of the plant. In 1611 the imports of tobacco from

Virginia were reduced to 142,085 pounds, one-sixth of the quantity previously exported to England." On this amazing statement we remark: (1) The above tax was ordered by James October 17, 1604, through the High Treasurer, the Earl of Dorset, but Parliament gave it no sanction and in 1613 this abject monarch farmed out the tobacco duties for the sole benefit of the Crown. (2) The first European to cultivate tobacco in Virginia was John Rolf who began the work in his garden at Jamestown in 1612. No exportation of tobacco from Virginia to England is recorded before 1619. (3) The hard times in Virginia and Maryland were not primarily the result of duties on their tobacco but were due to their stupidity in producing nothing but tobacco, to competition with the superior Spanish products, and to tobacco production in England. In spite of all this the exports of tobacco from Virginia to England rose from 20,000 pounds in 1619 to 1,500,000 pounds in 1629. (4) That England was very arbitrary in holding the trade of her colonies is illustrated in Sir John Pennington's lawless seizure of the *White Greyhound* of Rotterdam, laden with colonial tobacco and cotton. Sir

John felt sure that the government would take a reasonable view of the episode as it would bring to the impecunious Charles I at least a thousand pounds. England owes to America the development of her sea power. Returning to James, here is a specimen of his polemics against smoking: "A custom lothsome to the eye, hateful to the nose, harmful to the braine, dangerous to the lungs, and in the black stinking fume thereof, neerest resembling the horrible Stygian smoke of the pit that is bottomlesse." There is little evidence that James, claiming to be the vice-regent of God with plenary divine rights, realised his powerlessness in the presence of Nicotiana. The *Birmingham Daily Post* of December 16, 1870, probably expresses an enlightened opinion when it says: "In his insular ignorance, King James never knew that some form of narcotic had been smoked and snuffed and chewed, by all tribes and in all ages of the world. He wrote his 'counterblast,' and in his royal conceit doubtless thought he had 'put out the light' in England and in Europe too." The upshot of the matter in England was that the stupid policy of prohibition was abandoned, and tobacco as a royal

[59]

monopoly became one of the most fruitful revenue producers of the realm. There are limitations to the powers of courts and governments,
but not to their pretensions and stupidities.

Meanwhile interesting developments were
going on in France. In 1610, Louis XIII, son
of Henry IV, came to the throne disgusted with
the smoking habits of the court. Of course he
found the nobility and the clergy in full agree-
ment with him. He regarded smoking as un-
dignified and offensive, especially among the
ladies of the court, but was too wise to prohibit
the practise by edict. The custom of puffing
was gradually changed to snuffing, as being far
more dainty and elegant. Thus arose and flour-
ished snuffers and snuff boxes, under the suf-
ferance of Louis himself, yet under the
patronage of both church and state, for the
priesthood was already more inclined toward
snuff. Richelieu, who became Louis's Minister
in 1624, was like his king very unfriendly to
tobacco, but he saw clearly that to prohibit tobacco would be a practical failure and would
at the same time deprive the state of important
revenue. In 1635 Louis XIII restricted the
sale of tobacco to apothecaries and then only by

prescription from a physician. He saw, what James I could not see, that arbitrary sumptuary laws are sure to fail and to weaken respect for more fundamental laws. Thus there grew up in France a system of tobacco control by taxation and supervision which with perturbations exists to-day as a state monopoly. It is interesting to note that Benjamin Franklin in 1777 borrowed two million louis from the *fermiers général*, holders of the French tobacco monopoly, by agreeing to deliver Virginia tobacco.

Louis XIV was like James I in two respects only. He hated tobacco in every form and could say, "L'état c'est moi." He had an enormous appetite for foods and funds and a good digestion for both. He farmed out the taxes and lavished the proceeds upon kingly magnificence. During his reign (1643-1715) snuffing grew as a courtly exercise throughout Europe, and the goldsmiths were busy in devising snuff boxes for the élite which should be more in harmony with the splendour of *le Roi Soleil*. He tried to eliminate snuff-taking from his court, and the royal physician Fagon is said to have made a public oration against snuffing, but failed to convince his audience because in the violence of his onslaught he occasionally refreshed himself with a pinch of the hateful dust. But smoking continued to some extent within the court. Miss Pardoe in her *History of the Court of Louis XIV* shows that the daughters of the *Grand Monarque* occasionally held a smoking orgy in their own apartments after supper, with pipes borrowed from the officers of the Swiss guard. Still, a prejudice against smoking seems to have existed in French court circles to the time of Napoleon. Corti relates that Napoleon, who from his youth up was a mighty snuff taker, told the smoking Prince of Hesse-Darmstadt, "If you come to Paris with your clothes smelling of smoke not a woman will look at you." This is a very extravagant statement about Paris, but it indicates a certain court dislike of smoking.

The opposition to the use of tobacco on the part of the church seems to have been amply justified, and perhaps unduly delayed. It appears that some of the Catholic missionaries in the New World, especially in Peru, had become so intemperate and bad-mannered as to take their snuffing, chewing, and smoking into the churches and even into the celebration of the mass, to the scandal of the people they were sent to serve. Similar outrages of decency were perpetrated in Spain, particularly in Seville, and also in some of the Italian cities. On the ground of many complaints, Pope Urban VIII in 1624 issued a bull in which he says, "Tobacco has gained so strong a hold on persons of both sexes, yea, even priests and clerics, that—We blush to state—during the actual celebration of Holy Mass, they do not shrink from taking tobacco through the mouth or nostrils, thus soiling the altar linen and infecting the churches with its noxious fumes. * * * All persons thus offending shall be punished by immediate excommunication, etc." His successor, Innocent X, in 1650 interdicted the use of tobacco in any form in St. Peter's Church under penalty of instant excommunication.

The net result in western Europe of the opposition of church and state to tobacco was negligible. On the whole, snuffing gained in popularity on account of its relative safety, simplicity, and decency. The state found that sumptuary prohibition did not prohibit, and turned its attention to revenue from tobacco, often taking special concessions for the Crown.

[63]

The church was equally powerless, with her excommunications perforated by loopholes. In 1655 she gave up the fight, farmed out tobacco and brandy, and gave her attention to revenue for the Papal States. As the church at first rejected Aristotle but finally glorified him as the wisest of all philosophers, so her early opposition to tobacco culminated in the use of snuff by several of her supreme pontiffs. Thus about the middle of the seventeenth century church and state came to the same conclusion regarding the tobacco problem, abandoning both prohibition and excommunication.

CHAPTER IV

MODES OF PRODUCTION AND CONSUMPTION OF SNUFF

FOR an indefinite period the production of snuff in Europe followed the methods of the native Americans. This means in part that the variously cured tobacco leaves were treated by hand or in a mortar with pestle. But as Spain became acquainted with Central America, and Portugal with Brazil, it is reasonable to suppose that the more refined methods of the culture of Montezuma, and of the Indians of the Orinoco, were adopted. This would mean the introduction of hand mills, of containers and of various scents or aromas in snuff production. Later, Seville became the emporium for snuff, and it was probably here that the first differentiations in curing, preparing, scenting and packing tobacco were worked out. With the growth of snuffing, factories sprang up throughout the world. Chambers, in his *Encyclopædia*, 1727, says, "The kinds of snuff and their several names are infinite." To this we add nothing. The adulterations of snuff were as numerous as its varieties. The flavour of tobacco was often destroyed through washings and scents and sometimes the tobacco itself was eliminated by substitutes. The history of snuff production is almost as intricate as that of wine making. Let the reader consider the great variety of tobacco plants, of soils and climates, modes of cultivation and cure, of ways of packing and time of fermentation, of temperatures, mixtures, and scents in manufacturing—we shall then be excused for giving but two simple examples. As stated by Billings, the recipe for making a popular snuff named "Maroco" is: "Take forty parts of French or St. Omar tobacco with twenty parts of fermented Virginia stalks in powder; the whole to be ground and sifted. To this powder must be added two pounds and one-half of rose leaves in fine powder; and the whole must be moistened with salt and water and thoroughly incorporated. After that it must be worked up with cream and salts of tartar, and packed in lead to preserve its delicate aroma." The celebrated *gros grain* Paris snuff is composed of "equal parts of Amersfoort and James River tobacco, and the scent is imparted by a 'sauce,' among the ingredients of which are salt, soda, tamarinds, red wine, syrup, cognac, and cream of tartar." It is interesting to compare these eighteenth-century productions with those of the Brazilian Indians in the sixteenth century as found in our first chapter.

Within the frame of the larger picture of snuff production we should notice the snuff-mill and the grater, which were early used by the pharmacist dispenser of snuff or by private persons. For these devices tobacco leaves were pressed or curled into plugs, *carottes*, pigtails, and twists of different forms and sizes. The mills passed through the mortar stage into small grinding mills similar to those used later for coffee. The graters, rasps, or rappees appear in different sizes, ranging from two or three inches for the pocket to twelve or sixteen inches for family use. The terms *carotte* and *rappee* take us back to about 1600, when tobacco for snuff was prepared in the form of a carrot to be rasped as wanted. Thus we have *Tabac râpé*, or *rappee* or *grated tobacco* and its attendant snuff rasp-box. The best graters had a cover of ivory,

[67]

wood, or metal, elaborately ornamented, painted, or engraved, rivalling in workmanship their later successful competitors, the ornate snuff boxes. Graters have become very rare but are sometimes found in museums. A small pocket grater in my collection is contained in a silver cylinder about two inches long, with hinges at either end, and is in perfect adjustment, combining *carotte*, grater, and snuff container. I am a bit skeptical about the "nutmeg-grater" which the English Puritan carried in his travels "to satisfy an individual taste, as mulled wine, or negus was a night cap," and which the New England Puritan carried "to season food when travelling." The Reverend George Whitefield, "who thrilled his vast audiences by his eloquence and powerful rich voice," owned one of these. The fact that the pocket nutmeg grater and the snuff grater appeared and disappeared together in time is as interesting as the possibility that our fathers of the eighteenth century indulged the nutmeg luxury. My suspicion is that the container held neither a "wooden nutmeg" nor a real one but a *carotte* of Virginia tobacco, which yields the rich brown dust that might be mistaken for nutmeg.

When Schopenhauer was reproved for abusing "God's chosen people," he laconically remarked, "Tastes differ." Some might think this is a rather impious application of the old axiom *de gustibus non est disputandum,* but it expresses the truth not only in the general realm of the fine arts but also in those mysterious regions of taste and smell that have been so strangely neglected in the field of æsthetics, and which tobacco has partially explored. The multiplicity of kinds, scents, containers, and names of snuff was partly due to "variety is the spice of life" or *chacun à son gout* and partly to the effort of producers to stimulate consumption by new labels or nomenclature. The rejuvenating power of new names for old things or processes is very great. Thus we feel quite *au fait* in psychology and sociology when we learn that psycho-analysis gives rise to behaviorism and this in turn to mental and cultural complexes, and that Europe took over from America the tobacco complex, the potato complex, and the maize complex.

Snuff played a considerable social rôle for

about three hundred years in the life of all peoples. It broke the ice of silence in all gatherings and furnished an unlimited field for conversation and controversy. It stimulated friendships and made new conquests, as well as revealed human attitudes and manners.

What introduces Whig or Tory,
And reconciles them in their story,
When each is boasting in his glory?
      A pinch of snuff.

Where speech and tongue together fail,
What helps old ladies in their tale,
And adds fresh canvas to their sail?
      A pinch of snuff.

One of the social customs may be referred to in an amusing anecdote. After a dinner in Portman Square the snuff boxes made their appearance, and that of Beau Brummell was much admired. One guest found it hard to open and applied a dessert knife to the lid. Brummell was on thorns, and finally addressed his host with suavity, "Will you be good enough to tell your friend that my snuff box is not an oyster?"

Stewart as quoted by Billings sees in the consumption of snuff a philosophy of history and a benefactor of humanity. His view is that when we consider the beneficial influence which snuff has exercised over mankind generally, we can not help regretting that its virtues were not sooner known. "For we put forth the proposition seriously," says Stewart, "that its effect upon the world has been to render it more humane and even-tempered, and that had the western hemisphere discovered the tobacco plant earlier, historians would have had more pleasant events to chronicle. It is most probable that the fate of Rome, discussed by the triumvirate over their snuff boxes would have been different." After reviewing many historical events, and claiming that the great deeds of great men who were snuff takers may be traced to this dearly prized luxury he remarks: "My hypothesis may seem an absurd one, but history supports it." He believes that snuff civilised Scotland and produced her many great men of the eighteenth century. Had Stewart lived until our day he would explain present depressions and political stupidities by the abandonment of the snuff box.

[71]

The snuffer had an æsthetic advantage of the smoker, as he was not dependent on the tinder-box with its steel, flint, and punk, or on the sputtering candle, or the coals of the fire pot. Among the élite the manner of handling the snuff box, and the correct way of conveying the titillating dust to the expectant nostrils, were of the utmost importance. Schools were formed to this end; one in London added to its snuff curriculum, instruction in the proper use of the fan. Thus Pope writes:

Snuff or the fan supply each pause of chat
With singing, laughing, ogling and all that.

An advertisement in the *Spectator*, August 8, 1711, reads, "The exercise of the Snuff Box, according to the most fashionable Airs and Notions in opposition to the exercise of the Fan will be taught with the best plain or perfumed Snuff, at Charles Lillis's & C." After the snuff box was drawn from the pocket by the left hand, the fingers of the right hand gave the cover three taps, then the box was opened and a pinch of snuff placed on the back of the left hand or on the thumb-nail enclosed by the forefinger, and so inhaled. But generally the pinch of snuff went directly to the nose—and elsewhere in careless addicts. The why of the three taps, which was almost universal, is not known. It is not necessary to refer it to any triad, or trinity, or to the "God bless you" after the sneeze. The sneeze, like most omens, has different and even opposite meanings in time and place. Catullus tells us that when Cupid sneezed

The little loves that waited by,
Bowed and blessed the augury.

The mannerisms of snuffing were sure to excite the interest of the satirists, even on the part of those masters who were not strangers to its charms. Thus Stewart says that Steele, whose weakness for dress and show was proverbial, levelled many of his blunt shafts at its use; while Pope, who himself tells us of his "wig all powdered and all snuff his band" let fly one of his keener arrows at the beaux whose wit lay in their snuff boxes. But of all satirists of snuffing none can compare with John Heinrich Cohausen who in his *Lust of the Longing Nose*, 1720, writes: "Do but notice what grimaces snuff takers make, how their whole features are convulsed, how they dip into their snuff boxes in measured rhythm, cock up their noses, compose their mouths, eyes, and all their features to a pompous dignity, and, as they perform the solemn rite of snuff-taking, they look as if they scorned the whole world, or were bent on some enterprise of which they might say, like Bouflet, 'I will make the whole world tremble!'" Here the æsthetically neglected nose rises to a dramatic dignity commensurate with its position in the human physiognomy. But we may turn from this sarcastic abstraction to the concrete and caressing experience of the poet:

> *Knows he that never took a pinch—*
> *Nosey!—the pleasure thence which flows?*
> *Knows he the titillating joy—*
> *Which my nose knows?*
>
> *O nose!—I am as proud of thee*
> *As any mountain of its snows!*
> *I gaze on thee and feel that pride*
> *A Roman knows!*

The use of the tiny spoon, such as are found in Chinese snuff bottles, was not uncommon in

Europe, especially among women. Thus we have the complaint:

To such a height with some is fashion grown
They feed their very nostrils with a spoon.

This device had the advantages of keeping the nails clean, and of excluding other people's nails and noses from one's powder.

Snuffing had so many psychical aspects of status and attitude that an attempt has been made to classify them. Thus we have the pinch military as with Frederick the Great and Napoleon, the pinch malicious of Pope, the pinch dictatorial of Ben Jonson, the pinch sublimely contemptuous of Reynolds, and the pinch polite of Talleyrand. The latter held snuff-taking to be essential to politicians, as it gives time for thought in answering awkward questions while pretending only to indulge in a pinch.

Among the élite the snuff box was not more democratic than the toothbrush or the pipe. It might be *pro bono amico* but never *pro bono publico*. When someone took a pinch from the box of George II which was lying on the table, the king threw the box out of the window. Frederick the Great, discovering a page purloining a pinch from his box, exclaimed: "Boy, put that box in your pocket; it is not large enough for both of us." Lord X, visiting his tailor, laid his box on the counter, whereupon the tailor took a pinch. Lord X remarked, "Since we are equals you are no longer my tailor," and walked out of the shop. Still, we are warned not to generalise for both sexes, as Addison complains in the *London Spectator* that a lady of fashion too often pulls out her box full of good Brazile in the middle of the sermon; and to show she has the audacity of a well-bred woman offers it to the men as well as the women who sit near her. The serio-comic aspect of the habit is shown by the Scotch clergyman who, running out of snuff, was miserable and unable to work until his clever servant, going to the kirk, swept up the dust about the pulpit and thus relieved the *malaise* of his master. Similar results would have been attained by shaking out the garments of Ben Jonson, or Swedenborg, or Lady Mary Wortley Montagu.

Because the spectacular snuff box has disappeared into museums and private collections before the all-conquering cloud of smoke, it is often inferred that snuff also has disappeared. Yet statistically the consumption of snuff is keeping pace with the growth of population. In these years of abnormal depression the three leading producers of snuff in the United States show combined earnings, production, and surplus for 1931 respectively of $7,084,601, 39,543,096 pounds, and $30,657,584. The chief mode of snuff consumption to-day is not snuffing, or dipping, or rubbing, or chewing, but soaking or holding it in the cheek with an occasional pressure. It is estimated that less than two percent of the snuff manufactured to-day enters the nostrils. There are still many species and sub-species of snuff—sweet, strong, and salt; plain, fine, and coarse; dry, semi-moist, and moist; scented with rose, lemon, verbena, or bergamot, etc. The spirit of advertising remains about the same, though differing a bit in letter, as may be seen by the statement of Samuel Major in the *General Advertiser*, London, June 21, 1749: "I have published my Imperial Snuff for all disorders in the head; and I think I might have gone farther, and said, for all disorders of body and mind." The banner

has passed in our day to the manufacturer of
the all-conquering cigarette, of which one may
say,

*Without joking, the cigarette is the poetry of
    smoking,*
And needs no constant stoking, as my pipe.
I like a good cigar, but my funds don't go so far
As for the cigarette, with even more delight.

CHAPTER V

FORM AND MATTER OF SNUFF CONTAINERS

THE containers of snuff include a great variety of pockets, bags, pouches, mulls, bottles, and boxes. The beginnings of all these are found among the American aborigines. The Indian custom of carrying tobacco in small animal skins or leather bags decorated with coloured thread or paints, and later with beads, has prevailed throughout the world even to our own day. In the Orient bags and pouches were suspended from the girdle, and were often beautifully ornamented, as may be seen in Persian and Turkish collections or in the exquisitely simple lac and Japan of the Far East.

Snuff bottles were not uncommon in Europe even in the seventeenth century. Bragge describes a Norwegian bottle of bone mounted with brass; brass stopper and chain; circles of brass on sides; on side initial G.E.S. and date 1647; dimensions 3½ x ⅞. Both table and pocket bottles seem to have been very popular in Norway and were made of wood, bone, horn, deer's hoof, amber, ivory, walrus tusk, silver and other metals. The decorations of many of these bottles with medallions, figures, and engravings show the value attributed to them. While in Germany and Italy some bottles were used, they never became widely popular, being less easily carried than the box. Of Chinese bottles we shall discourse later.

The word "mull" has its origin in the Scottish Highlanders' pronunciation of "mill," the name of the implement used for pulverising tobacco. A mull is generally of natural horn, with the small end often artificially curved and the larger end capped by bone, wood, or metal, often bearing in the centre a cairngorm or some other semi-precious stone. Dr. Mott, in a note to his edition of Dekker's *Gull's Hornbook*, says, "The Scotch mull, or sneeshing mull, was often accompanied by a spoon and hare's foot attached by chain, the one for applying snuff to the nose, the other for wiping the upper lip." More tools were appended by those who put great emphasis on the antecedents and consequences of snuffing. I have seen but two examples of the communal

[80]

or guild mull, one of which I possess. It is a
very large ram's horn with one and one-half
turns, the small end in plain silver, the large
end capped with an engraved silver box, on the
hinged lid of which is a rampant eagle one and
three-fourths inches high. The feet are in
turned silver, so that they may move easily about
the table. The length of the whole is ten
inches, the height eight inches, and the diam-
eter of the snuff box three and one-fourth
inches. The mull described by Bragge has mal-
let, pricker, rake, spoon, and hare's foot, all
attached by chains—evidently a private table
mull.

Snuff boxes vary in size from the tiny ones
carried by milady in hand or bag or on chate-
laine to the generous table and mantel boxes for
the benefit of the family and guests. It is reported that Frederick the Great had a snuff box
in every room in his palaces. If his other guests
were like Voltaire, an ample supply of snuff was
needed! It is said that Mary Lamb would put
a half-dozen small boxes in her bag and make
as many social calls, returning with her stock of
snuff quite replenished. The term snuff box is
somewhat ambiguous, as it belongs to that large

group of small boxes which includes the comfit, "bonbon," and "powder boxes." When snuffing arose, small boxes used for other purposes were probably requisitioned, and when the habit subsided the boxes were used according to the fancy of the possessor. Evidently many of the most valuable snuff boxes never contained snuff, but remained unsullied, as beautiful and cherished mementos. One knows a snuff box more by intuition than by definition. No classification of forms by periods is possible. It is idle to speak of the rounds of Louis XIV, or the ovals of Louis XV, or the rectangulars of Louis XVI. These are prevailing forms from Henry IV to Louis Philippe, and throughout this period nearly every geometrical form is probably represented. The oldest dated snuff box known is an oval in silver, of 1655, and Bragge describes one, in the form of a shell, done in copper, with the date 1662. The older snuff boxes are very rarely dated. By analogies as well as by direct evidence we may be sure that throughout the seventeenth and eighteenth centuries the artists worked with freedom, not only in form, but in material, colour, and decoration. Still, it was not until the time of the French Revolution and subsequent years that inventions really ran riot in the field of form. Here we have hats, caps, shoes, boots, human and animal heads and figures, fishes, turtles, flies, bellows, fans, pistols, and what not. I have a mutilated copy of the legendary Devonshire Pistol, made to shoot snuff into the nostrils. There are also boxes with false or double inner tops or bottoms; boxes with secret portraits or erotic paintings; screw, spring, and slip boxes or the puzzle sort; and boxes with double lids and containers, insuring both public and private use.

My collection contains a Spanish applewood box with five lids and containers—top, bottom, ends, and one side—yet in measurement only four and three-fourths by two and three-fourths inches. The hinges are of wood, and the whole so perfectly made as to be water tight, with jointures almost invisible.

Psychological crotchets are not of our day only—for form, colour, and decoration of the snuff box were at one time thought to be more significant of character than clothes. Early in the eighteenth century a contributor to the *Tatler* writes, "I will call at Bubbleboy's shop and find out the shape of the fellow's snuff box,

by which I can settle his character." This
enigma must have been a very ordinary fellow;
otherwise he would have had at least a half-
dozen containers. It was quite common to have
a different box for every day of the week, and
for very special occasions. Still, individual taste
played a great rôle in ordinary life, while among
the élite there was more uniformity in material
and decoration—engraved and ornamented gold
boxes probably taking the lead.

In respect to the materials for snuff boxes,
the mineral, vegetable, and animal realms have
responded bounteously, both in their simplicity
and in combination. All the minerals are represented, from platinum, gold and crystal to
lead and iron. The vegetable products are represented by almost every kind of wood, bamboo,
gourd, and amber. The lower forms of animal
life yield all sorts of shells, the queen of which
is the pearl oyster, and its rival for the throne,
the amphibian tortoise. The higher animals
have furnished leather, bones, horns, tusks, and,
the king of all animal products, ivory, which is
not only beautiful in itself but takes colours with
brilliancy, and has challenged by its fine grain
the skill of artists and engravers since the early

Egyptian dynasties. Though the origins of painting on ivory go back to an indefinitely early date, it is to Richard Cosway of the eighteenth century that we owe the perfecting of this technique. For many years Cosway did miniature work on snuff boxes for leading goldsmiths. Then about 1761 he began independent portrait work on ivory, and soon became the most popular miniaturist in England, at the very time when Reynolds, Gainsborough, Romney, Raeburn, Lawrence, and Hoppner were glorifying portraiture on canvas. A good idea of the boxes of Queen Anne's time is given in *Pandora's Box; a Satyr Against Snuff*, published in 1719:

For females fair and formal fops to please,
The mines are robb'd of ore, of shells the seas,
With all that Mother Earth and beast afford
To man, unworthy now, tho' once their lord;
Which wrought into a box, with all the show
Of art the greatest artists can bestow,
Charming in shape, with polish't rays of light,
A joint so fine it shuns the sharpest sight,
Must still be graced with all the radiant gems
And precious stones that ere arrived in Thames.

Within the lid the painter plays his part,
And with his pencil proves his matchless art;
There drawn to life some spark or mistress
*   dwells,*
Like hermits chaste and constant to their cells.

To all these natural materials for snuff boxes
we must add such composites as glass, porcelain,
and *papier-mâché*, which, though not ornamented with pearls and precious stones, are not
less artistic and brilliant in their choicest examples. To these materials, including tortoise
shell, a more detailed emphasis should be given.

The shield of the tortoise is formed in very
thin layers or shingles about three times as long
as their breadth. These layers are easily soft-
ened by heat and may be welded together in any
shape or thickness required. Unlike ivory, tortoise shell seldom cracks, checks, or warps
in changing temperatures. These remarkable
qualities, to which must be added fine texture
and translucent colours, render it very desirable
for decoration and engraving. Tortoise shell
played a considerable rôle in the fine arts of the
Orient, long before it entered Europe where it
was given varied expression by Boule in Paris

and Laurentini in Naples. Boule used the shell chiefly for inlay work on larger pieces, while Laurentini developed the finer inlays of gold which gave rise to marquetries, to the *posé d'or* of silhouettes, and to the *piqué d'or* of the very delicate gold-point inlays that form many beautiful designs on shell snuff boxes. The heavier work of this latter sort takes the name of *clouté d'or*. I have a snuff box in which the relief carving of human figures and trees is as excellent as any similar work done in ivory; and also other tortoise shell boxes decorated with gold in the styles mentioned, including marquetry and guilloche, which show how exquisite are the two materials in combination. It has been said that the more ancient shell boxes are light in colour. I doubt this statement because this is the colour of my box, whereon is depicted, in chased gold associated with *piqué d'or*, a balloon ascension, Paris, 1773; and another box of the same period of Louis XVI, in the Piogey collection in Paris, is in *posé d'or* on light shell. My carved box already mentioned is in dark shell, and supposed to be older than the light one. Probably a time classification of colour is as arbitrary as that of form.

Papier-mâché has given us more snuff boxes than any other single material, a fact which arises from the number of its peculiar merits. It is the lightest, and at the same time one of the most durable of materials. It never cracks, checks, or warps. It keeps the snuff cool and moist better than any other container except lead. It takes a very fine finish, giving an excellent ground for the painter's skill. It lends itself agreeably to all such prints as are held by paste and varnish. For all these reasons, the range of value is very great, and depends primarily on the quality of decoration and varnishing. *Papier-mâché* is a synthesis of the finest paper paste, lacquer or gum arabic, and china clay. This synthesis is moulded or pressed into the desired form, lacquered, finished with rotten stone for decoration, and then given a final varnish.

Much mystery hangs about the lacquers and varnishes, notwithstanding John Stalker's *Treatise of Japanning and Varnishing, being a Complete Discovery of those Arts*, published in London, 1688. What we do not know about the brilliant varnishes of the eighteenth century would be very interesting. It is said they were developed and carried to great perfection in Japan. Thither China sent her workmen to learn the secrets of the art, preparatory to the making of the Ti-Tscheon lacquers of Peking. With lacquer the indebtedness of China to Japan apparently begins and ends. Japan's snuff boxes are almost wholly confined to the lower vegetable world and to lacquer. They are much less interesting than the little button, toggle, or *netsuke* at the end of the cord which attaches the box or *inró* to sash or belt. These are often grotesque and charming—among them may be found all sorts of tiny human and animal figures cleverly carved from ivory, illustrating the daily lives, occupations, and beliefs of the people. Why this æsthetic contrast of China and Japan? Until recently Japan was relatively isolated, China open; Japan is probably southwestern Asiatic; China Mongolian; the soul of Japan is reflected in the simple Shinto worship and in Bushida, "the way of the Samurai," an intense fearless nationalism; China is essentially metaphysical, with her Confucius, Lao-tse, and Mencius. If comparisons are odious, contrasts are apt to be even more so. I am fully aware that each of the above propositions is debatable

[89]

and that the Japanese of all peoples in history have made the most sudden and cataclysmic change to western modernism while conservative China is still tumultuously waiting to be born. I am also inclined to the view that such beloved and overworked terms as "Race," "Heredity," and "Environment" are superficial fictions which invite loquacity and darken understanding, much as did those old refuges of ignorance, "Turanian," and "Aryan."

But let us return to Europe and to the mystery of *Vernis Martin*. About 1740 Etienne and Robert Martin went from Germany to Paris, where they joined a paper maker named Lefevre and began to produce *papier-mâché* snuff boxes. About 1744 Vernis Martin, under the patronage of the Crown, became known throughout Europe, and before 1764 it was considered a mark of distinction to own a Vernis Martin snuff-box. The Martins had succeeded in making a durable, translucent, and brilliant varnish; they also had secured the best artists to do their work on *papier-mâché*, wood, ivory, and certain metals. Perhaps, like Joseph Strass of Vienna, whose paste became famous in French jewelry about 1750, they brought their secret with them to Paris. Proof of the high contemporary esteem in which their work was held is shown by a payment by Louis XVI to Robert of about 15,460 *livres* for decorative workers at Versailles, and by the fact that their lacquer snuff boxes sold readily at the then enormous price of twenty-four to thirty *livres* each, while their *étuis*, fans, *carnets*, and *bonbonnières* commanded corresponding prices. The secret of Vernis Martin passed with Robert's death into the realm of lost arts, there to join the Egyptian Nile blue and the ruby red. Meanwhile Johann Heinrich Stobwasser, born in 1740, was developing a new lacquer product under the patronage of the Duke of Brunswick, and in 1772 the Stobwasser factory was opened in Berlin. Here too the best artists were secured, and decoration of a high order in portraiture, landscape, and *genre* was produced. These boxes, mostly in *papier-mâché*, are known as Braunschweig or Stobwasser, and on account of their superior varnish and excellent workmanship are very desirable.

In entering upon the relation of snuff boxes and bottles to the field of ceramics we find ourselves in a realm of vagaries and controversy.

Here we come at once upon "crystal glass," which, like "psycho-physics," seems a contradiction in terms. I am sure the crystal would say to the glass: "I was formed in nature's great laboratory through millions of years and with definite structure, while you are a synthetic, amorphous stuff made in the laboratories of man; I am quartz, diamond, ruby, sapphire, emerald, while you are nothing but a pasty imitation of my everlasting qualities." Of course the crystal is right, and all the glories of glass, and glaze, and enamel, and porcelain must admit their human origins and inheritances. All these are essentially of one family, having as their physical background a synthesis of sand, potash, and oxide of lead, however much they may differ as æsthetic products by variations and additions, and by the introduction of other metallic oxides for purposes of colour.

Concerning the origin of pottery, glass, glazes, and soft pastes we know nothing. Like fire, the wheel, the wedge, and the lever, they are beyond the horizon of history. We know that the potter's wheel was working in the fourth Egyptian dynasty, about 3,800 years B.C., that glass was manufactured in Mesopotamia and Egypt, 2500 B.C., and that a glass factory was established in China by Wu-ti of the Han dynasty, 140 B.C. This last event, moreover, had been preceded by hundreds of years of excellent Chinese work in porcelain and bronze.

The general type, as to size and form, of the Chinese snuff bottle, which was fixed for snuff with spoon, cork, and semi-precious stone cap in the Ming dynasty, 1368-1644, apparently antedates the Christian era. Many specimens of Chinese decorated porcelain bottles have been found in Egypt at Thebes, Sakkarah, and Ghiseh, possibly dating as early as 1500 B.C., showing, like the Tel-el-Amarna tablets, Egyptian intercourse with the East. The discoveries of Layard and Cesnola, as well as the seventeen specimens now in the museum of the New York Historical Society, seem to establish a direct or indirect relation of Egypt with Cathay. As bottles of this type were widely used for perfumes, scents, medicines, and opiates, the Oriental taste for these explains their wide distribution and their later adaptation to snuff. The Portuguese were in Asiatic waters as early as 1511; a little later Magellan was in the Philippines, and in

1537 the Portuguese established the first European colony in the Far East at Macao, on the confines of China. Tobacco was introduced to China about this time, and soon after snuffing seems to have become the favourite form of its consumption. We might call the period from 1537-1644 one of adaptation of the bottle to the uses of snuff while the great period of the snuff bottle *floruit* in production, reproduction, and trade is that of the Manchu dynasty, 1644-1912, with its leading emperors K'ang Hsi, Yung Chêng, and Ch'ien Lung, and its development of the great centre of fine ceramic production in China, Ching-te Chen. Perhaps the more outstanding work began under Ch'ien Lung about 1736. Still, names do not limit the production of snuff bottles, in which the Chinese patience and skill have so completely expressed themselves. The glass bottles show such a variety of glazes, colours with their combinations, imitations of semi-precious stones, and cameo cuttings as to beggar description. Bragge lists thirteen snuff boxes in imitation of mochastone and agate said to be made by the use of the silex of the rice plant. The layers of glass in cameo are sometimes undercut, which adds to

[94]

the brilliancy of the superior figures and symbols. It is said that eight figures express love, luck, fame, and immortality, and are sometimes called Buddhistic emblems. But the mysterious Chinese symbolism shall not detain us. The more interesting and elaborate bottles made of vitreous pastes and done in high relief are attributed to the great artist Hu of Peking.

Of all Chinese bottles the most exquisite, mysterious, and highly prized are those in which the painting and lettering is made on the inside of the bottle by the artist. The origin of inside painting has been attributed to the greatest of all Chinese artists, Wu Tao-Tzu of the T'ang dynasty, who worked the miracle in quartz or crystal. Laufer says the inside of the bottle is treated with pulverised iron oxydul mixed with water, which, shaken for a half day, forms a milk-white coating suitable for receiving paints. The artist lies on his back holding the bottle up to the light between the thumb and index finger of the left hand. "The hairy tip of the brush is not straight, as usual, but stands under a right angle against the handle." His eyes are constantly fixed on the outer surface of the glass, thus watching the gradual development of the picture as it emerges from under the glass. He first outlines a skeleton sketch in black ink, starting from below and then passing on to the middle and sides, finally inserting the colours. This art industry commenced in the K'ien-Lung period, 1736-95, and the little masterpieces turned out at that time are unsurpassed. The modern output is chiefly intended for the foreign market, and does not stand comparison with the products of bygone days; the bottles are large, coarse, and clumsy, and the paintings are usually crude.

Precious stones and pearls very rarely appear as decorations in Chinese snuff bottles, yet Bragge lists a bottle in brown chalcedony with a large ruby as a stopper cap, and a glass bottle "incrusted with groups of pearls, which the Chinese cause the pearl oyster to secrete in the form desired." The pocket or sash bottles range from two inches to three and one-half inches in height, while the table bottles are from three and one-half inches to four and one-half inches.

It is interesting to note that the decline of snuffing in the Orient and Occident was synchronous. After the period of Tao Kuang, 1821-1850, the bottle and box seldom graced the hand, sash, or pocket of the Chinese *élite*. While the Chinese snuff bottle was rarely used in the Western world for the pocket, there seems to have been a good trade in Europe and America in glass table bottles of various colours, some of which are now regarded as very desirable, especially those with the original labels. About 1769 Richard Wister in New Jersey and a little later Thomas Leiper of Philadelphia are said to have made a few pocket bottles. I have a small pear-shaped glass bottle, with an acorn screw cap at the small end and a full screw bottom, lined with cork for filling. Bottles of wood and leather are more common, however. While there are many public and private collections of Chinese snuff bottles in Europe and America, the Metropolitan Museum of New York City is fortunate in possessing three, the Altman, the Bishop, and the Converse collections, which taken together give an excellent idea of the materials, form, sizes, colours, engravings, paintings, and cameo work of the choicest field of Chinese art. The Altman collection is especially interesting for the variety of material and excellence of workmanship displayed. Among the one hundred and seventy-one specimens in hard stone are found bottles of agate, agalatolite, alabaster, aquamarine, bloodstone, carnelian, chalcedony, crystal, jasper, lapis-lazuli, malachite, sardonyx, serpentine, tourmaline, and turquoise, many marvellously carved or engraved.

The relation of the snuff box to the ceramics of the Western world opens a very large field concerning which only a few words are necessary. Brevity of treatment does not imply that the best porcelain and enamel snuff boxes with their metal mountings are not very desirable to museums and collectors. The hard porcelain paste, a synthesis of kaolin and feldspar, was first produced at Meissen in Saxony in 1710 and was put on sale at the Leipzig fair in 1715. Though preceded by many hundreds of years in the Orient, this was an outstanding event in Europe. The Capo di Monte factory began operation in 1743, and its small boxes done in the style of the Chinese Te-Hwa were much prized. A little later factories began appearing in all parts of Europe, and England in particular became an important center, boasting its famous Bow, Chelsea, Battersea, and Wedgwood. Bragge lists five bottles of Chinese porcelain which closely resemble in density, hardness, and polish the best specimens of Wedgwood's jasper ware. Horace Walpole was delighted with the Battersea enamels, and sent to his friend Richard Bentley "one of these new snuff boxes done on copper plate." In 1753 Louis XV and Madame de Pompadour removed the Vincennes factory to Sèvres; in 1761 hard paste products were added, and Sèvres soon became the rival of Meissen or Royal Dresden among the artifact lovers of Europe. The Pompadour period, 1753-1763, brought porcelain snuff boxes into great vogue among the ladies, who, if they followed the example of the mistress of Louis XV, had a different box for every day of the year. This remarkable development was hardly under way when Satan entered this ceramic Eden in the person of John Sadler, who invented printing on both hard and soft pastes in 1753 and successfully tempted the leading factories to increase and so cheapen their production. Whether this "Fall" was upward or downwards depends on whether we maintain an aristocratic or a democratic standard of judgment. The Liverpool prints are interesting, but they are the beginnings of a drift in the invention, imitation, and mass production which has eliminated handwork, workmanship, and the apprentice system at the same time that it has enabled the humblest housewife of to-day to furnish her home and table with prints and herself with "pearls and precious stones" at a cost (and quality) undreamed of in the day of Josiah Wedgwood and Flaxman.

CHAPTER VI

COLLECTING AND COLLECTIONS

THE impulse to collect objects of art or of
personal interest is one of the many by-products
of that element in human nature sometimes
called "sporting blood." This is not to be associated with the economic prevision and provi-
sion that in animal and human communities
support social life and institutions. It is an
æsthetic exercise and refinement that may be
said to develop from the contents of the healthy
small boy's pocket, variously specialised. Collecting, in its purity, is carried on just for the
fun of seeking and finding the desired and desirable object. Some urge, like Longfellow in
his *Evangeline*, that the pleasure is in the pursuing, while others, like Lotz, hold that the
continual whetting of the knife is irksome if
nothing is to be cut. But why attempt to render
disjunctive a unified process? We do not fish
in the bathtub nor in the stagnant pool. It is

the permanent possibility of finding the object that keeps the sportsman and the collector out of the *maison de santé*. To formulate such a definition is not to overlook the pleasures of pursuing, or the occasional disappointment felt in looking at the bagged game. In collectors there is a great variety of types, ranging from that of the man who collects just for fun to the one who, like some big game hunters, finances the expedition, or perhaps goes along with it to some interesting point of safety or general headquarters, and then does the real hunting by proxy. But to the normal collector the snuff box enters into his personal experience first ideally; then, when he has discovered it, and its price, the deliciously exciting and critical moment has arrived when Hamlet's "to be or not to be" is pitted against the aphorism "he who hesitates is lost."

One hundred and fifty years ago the collector of snuff boxes and snuff bottles had a comparatively easy task in selecting types and varieties. Then the artists and factories were many, and were vying with each other in supplying the demands of the great vogue. It is interesting that at the height of this fashion many saw in these tiny works of art "a thing of beauty and a joy forever," and that crowned heads found no mementos comparable to the snuff box. Jacquemart, one of the ablest critics of art, regards the snuff boxes of France as classic in their perfection, and he adds: "We should pardon an eccentricity of fashion which has furnished so many beautiful things." Perhaps all fashions are eccentric, but very few produce anything of permanent value. It was in this period that Sylvain Pons, according to Balzac the first collector of snuff boxes, made his selections, and the Duc de Richelieu his very choice collection. Frederick the Great was reported as having fifteen hundred boxes, some of which have been pictured and described in Martin Klar's *Die Tabatieren Frederichs des Grossen*. The Prince de Conti is said to have left to his heirs eight hundred boxes, while those of Napoleon are called "numberless." Many small private collections of snuff boxes must have been made at this time, as is witnessed by subsequent donations to public museums throughout Europe.

The best workmanship in boxes declined rapidly after the Napoleonic period, caused partly, at least, by the fact that, with the rapid rise of

democracy and its standardisation of the medio-
cre, personal vanities and ostentations were dis-
continued. The revolution of 1848 and the
abdication of Louis Philippe saw the vulgar
cheapening of boxes by prints, pastes, and inferior varnishes. This debacle was accompanied
by the invention of cheap and serviceable
matches, which stimulated first pipe smoking,
then the cigar, and finally the cigarette. The
snuff box and bottle have disappeared from
use; the beautifully carved pipe and the ornate
cigar- and cigarette-holder are rapidly following
the same gloomy path—and the consumption of
tobacco has become less picturesque than a quick
luncheon in a Canal Street cafeteria. No longer
milady holds the box that puts her at ease while
displaying her fair white arm and flashing
rings; instead she sells her picture to advertise
some new or old brand of tobacco. No longer
does my gentleman raise from its velvet bed the
artistic pipe or cigar-holder, but picks at a cello-
phane package, smokes his stupid briar often
upside-down, or from the identical enunciatory
organ manages simultaneously his cigar and his
conversation.

One might suppose that the disappearance of

the snuff box and bottle from public use would
be accompanied by their disappearance from
public interest. This would be true if men were
mere utilitarians and were not lovers of the old
and the beautiful. That the old or the antique
is a highly relative term is illustrated by the recent announcement that "the Old Snuff Mill in
the Bronx, erected in 1760, is being preserved
by the City of New York on account of its great
antiquity." Thus the collector is reminded that
the relativity of words and things to time and
space is of great significance. I have visited
antique shops the contents of which have not
transcended in time the surroundings of my
boyhood days, nor is this a macrobiotic confes-
sion.

The snuff box cannot at present pretend to a
proved antiquity much beyond the middle of
the seventeenth century, and there were comparatively few before 1740. Thus the field of
the collector is practically limited to the little
more than two hundred years of the *floruit* of
the bonafide snuff box, which cannot always be
distinguished from the popular *bonbonnière*.
Napoleon carried both, one containing the excit-
ant snuff, the other pellets to relieve his cough.

Remembering that Napoleon was one of the most intemperate of snuffers and that he suffered from occasional paroxysms of choking, one might enquire into the relation of his snuffing to Moscow and Waterloo. The brilliant Italian, Paolo Mantegazza, always "up to snuff," suggests that Napoleon might have saved his Empire had he been a smoker, since smoking steadies while snuffing impels. He also holds that "the influence of smoking and snuffing on politics and war is ascertainable."

The reference to Napoleon reminds one that the collector should harbour a healthy skepticism regarding the phrase "decorated with precious stones." Indeed, from the beginning of his venture he should adopt the motto, *Caveat emptor*. About the middle of the eighteenth century Strass pastes and other synthetic processes, as well as some "artificial crystals," excelled precious stones or natural crystals in actual colour and often in brilliancy. Even Napoleon, the collector of snuff boxes and the lover of brilliant decorations, presented to Captain Ussher at Elba, May 27, 1814, a finely engraved gold snuff box holding the emperor's miniature framed in paste brilliants, now in the Victoria and Albert Museum. If experts were divided in opinion on the material of the celebrated Portland Vase for more than two hundred years, some calling it agate, others sardonyx, and still others, like Montfaucon, a precious stone—all disfavoured by Josiah Wedgwood who in 1786 showed it to be glass—what is the value of the judgment of a novice to-day in the realm of natural and "artificial crystals" which parade themselves democratically or indistinguishably in every social status?

In the embellished boxes the jointures and especially the hinges tell most of the story. The least defect in workmanship in either of these may well arouse suspicion, in metal or porcelain or any other material. In all boxes printing and hand-coloured prints are a stumbling block to the novice, especially as regards the period from 1770 to about 1848, when public heroes and events were celebrated chiefly upon *papier-mâché* and porcelain boxes. But the collector does not "jest at scars" nor is he anxious to show them. He has the secret knowledge that experts, antique brokers, and museum curators are occasionally fellow sufferers. Probably the distinguished pieces of furniture that came to

America in the *Mayflower* are not much in excess of the number of snuff boxes made from Shakespeare's mulberry tree or Nelson's *Victory* or Napoleon's table at Waterloo.

Count Corti in his *History of Smoking* says, "If one could collect all Napoleon's snuff boxes in one room and arrange them in chronological order they would form a picture history of his life." One might suppose this statement a bit overdrawn, but in this particular period there is no higher authority.

The balloon exploits of the Montgolfier brothers, and the later use of the parachute in 1797, stimulated the imagination of artists, engravers, and printers to results quite as fruitful as did the events of the Napoleonic period. What a field for the collector with a *penchant* for biography and social history! Why not a review of French history from Louis XIV to Louis Philippe, or of English history from Elizabeth to Victoria, perhaps not merely in snuff boxes but in snuffing and smoking?

Through many years some of the finest collections of snuff boxes have found their way into public art museums and galleries. Among others there are the Lenoir-André-Rothschild cases in the Louvre, the Jones and Salting collections in the Victoria and Albert Museum, and the more extensive J. Pierpont Morgan exhibit in the Metropolitan Museum regarded by Sir Joseph Duveen as the most valuable collection in the world. These collections are made up of *élite* samples, which like the French court society have a certain ornate uniformity and monotony. While each piece is a gem deserving isolated study, the effect of the whole *en masse* is like a dinner where nothing is served but the most rare and expensive desserts. The gamut of taste is too abbreviated, and we feel the limitations of art rather than its freedom. For this reason some of the finer private collections are most interesting. But aside from questions of variety, and in spite of these large public collections, it may be confidently asserted that the greater number of good boxes are still in private hands or held as family heirlooms. The Hamilton family, for instance, possesses three snuff boxes of great historical interest; a choice, decorated, Meissen porcelain box given by Frederick the Great to Baron Steuben, who gave it to Alexander Hamilton; and two engraved gold snuff boxes, one belonging to

Hamilton, the other presented to Mrs. Hamilton by Talleyrand. But here again the virus of doubt assails the collector or possessor of the snuff box in the story of *Franklin's Patriotic Fib*, in the *North American Review* of June, 1932. Steuben was never more than a captain in the army of Frederick the Great and he left that service fourteen years before he sailed from France for America as "Lieutenant General in the service of the King of Prussia." Steuben, like Poor Richard, was a great man and a great actor, who added fresh laurels to the art of diplomacy while rendering inestimable service to the independence of America. Now and again the vicissitudes of life bring boxes to public attention and into the market. One of the most interesting private collections was that of Mr. C. H. T. Hawkins, who died at his home in Portland Place, London, in 1903. After his death numerous and valuable boxes were found scattered throughout the house and in bank vaults, many of them in original wrappers, unopened since their purchase. The collection has been gradually dissipated in Christie's auction rooms, and though a part remains unsold, several hundred thousands of pounds sterling have already been realised. Another illustration of how a private collection may come into the market is furnished by the very recent gold-selling rush in London, when forty gold snuff boxes were brought to a Piccadilly jeweler for melting, among them many fine examples of the Louis XV period. The boxes were saved from the melting pot and sold for fifteen thousand pounds sterling. This governmental urge of the melting pot reminds us of Cromwell, who ordered the silver statues of the twelve apostles of Winchester Cathedral to be minted into current coin, that they might "go about doing good like their Master." Cromwell was blind to the falsity of his analogy. How to keep civilisation out of the all-devouring melting pots of a sodden, soulless materialism is a permanent problem in human history. Fortunately the burial customs of ancient Egypt and Peru have preserved to us the unequalled craftsmanship of their goldsmiths. It is also well that the effacing fingers of time work chiefly on the surface of things. Boxes of various grades frequently pass through the markets, but good ones are rare. It is not uncommon in recent times to find a snuff box changing ownership at prices

ranging from two to ten thousand dollars. In
the March sale of 1904 Sir Joseph Duveen gave
£6,400, or about $32,000, for a Louis XV gold
snuff box by Hainelin. Even in the time of
George IV, we read in an account of money
expended at his coronation: "For snuff boxes to
foreign ministers, £8,295, 15s., 5d." I am sure
that the expenditures of crowned heads from
Louis XIV to George IV for snuff boxes would
reach an amazing figure. Two kings who dis-
liked tobacco in every form were protégés of
the box. Louis XIV employed the best goldsmiths and had studios erected for them in the
gardens of the Tuileries. In a study of Madame
de Pompadour by Marcelle Tinayre we are informed that Louis XV, being clever with his
hands, amused himself in cooking, turnery, and
fashioning snuff boxes. He made one of these
of firwood, unpeeled and hollowed out, which
was copied by professional craftsmen for the
New Year gifts of 1739.

From an artistic point of view the most expensive boxes are not always the most desirable.
One of the most costly snuff boxes known, containing three hundred and fifty-eight diamonds
and with a miniature exquisite in detail, fails to

satisfy through a maladjustment of its parts, the miniature being too large for the top and the ornamentation making the whole top-heavy. Neither cost nor ostentation is an æsthetic criterion.

Comparatively few boxes are signed by the artists but of those whose names are occasionally seen we may mention the von Blarenberghes, father and son (whose microscopic landscapes are almost as marvellous as the Chinese intrabottle paintings), Petitot, Watteau, Smart, Antoyne, Joaquet, Hall, Cooper, Cosway, Cheret, Neubert, Speth, Webber, Fragonard, Wieland, and Isabey; among the great enamellers are Petitot, Altaterre, Prevost, and Clavel. Many good copies from the older and greater artists are to be found on snuff boxes, as well as from such masters of *genre* as Teniers, van Ostade, Vermeer, Steen, and others.

Mere size does not function in pure mathematics and æsthetics. It is quite possible that a small snuff box may give greater satisfaction than a Tintoretto. As Williamson and Buckman remark in *The Art of the Miniature Painter:* "Miniature portraits may, in historical interest, often challenge comparison with large

[113]

oil paintings. Where, for example, can two large portraits be produced of greater historical interest than the two small highly-finished miniatures by Holbein, the portrait of Henry VIII sent to Anne of Cleves, and the returned one from Anne?" Of course most people like to make both little and big things look bigger, but much would often be gained by occasionally looking through an inverted telescope. The revelations of the microscope may be more wonderful than those of the telescope, and the microbe that swims in our blood may be more significant for humanity than the planet Jupiter.

Then why not economise time and space by an art gallery of Chinese bottles or French boxes? Chinese art expresses itself beautifully and completely in the snuff bottles, and the same may be said of French art in the eighteenth century as regards snuff boxes. What larger piece of French art in any century could command the price of Napoleon's gold snuff box with its miniatures of himself, Marie Louise, and the King of Rome done by Isabey? These little hand-pieces are emancipated from frames, pedestals, and walls. By a simple manipulation they tell their stories, of form and matter, of idea and artistry, in any light and at any time. They are more intimate, and personal, and companionable than any other form of art save perhaps the old engraved hunting case watch, which may rival the boxes with its inner inscriptions and pictures and its satisfying appeal to the sense of touch, which psychologically is perhaps the most fundamental of all sense-perceptional pleasures.

The famous Westminster snuff box has been regarded by Reginald Myer as "the most wonderful box that ever existed." It is of horn, oval in form, and made for the pocket. In 1713 Mr. Henry Mouck purchased it at the Horn Fair, held at Charlton in Kent, for the munificent sum of fourpence. Later he presented it to the Past Overseers Society of the Parishes of St. Margaret and St. John the Evangelist in the City of Westminster. The Society ornamented it with a silver rim engraved with the donor's name, and committed it to the custody of the Senior Overseer, who was to have recorded or symbolised on the box the outstanding event of the year, before turning it over to his successor. Thus every year brought a new event and a new artist to the task. When more space was needed a new case for the original was devised, until, as the product of more than two centuries, there has resulted a box of boxes, containing a chronological history of the Society of England, and of some of her best artists. There are miniature engravings of kings and statesmen, including one of the Duke of Cumberland of Culloden fame, 1746, by William Hogarth. A dramatic event occurred during the annual meeting of the Overseers in 1805, when news was received of the victory at Trafalgar and of the death of Nelson. The chairman arose and proposed the toast, "The Immortal Memory of Nelson." In every succeeding annual meeting to the present time the same toast has been given and, as then, drunk in silence. Quite as dramatic and more epic is the annual appearance of the Westminster box with all its trappings, especially when we remember that the heart of this venerated and priceless possession is a horn snuff box which originally cost fourpence, now holding within its lid the work of another immortal—Hogarth.

CHAPTER VII

REVIEW OF SELECTED LITERATURE

THE literature on tobacco, smoking and pipes is very extensive, but regarding snuff, snuffers, and snuff containers it is surprisingly meagre. A few general works bearing upon our subject may be noted.

Allemagne, H. D. d'. *Les accessoires du costume et du mobilier*. Paris, 1928. 3 vols. Includes an excellent review of snuff box production, with photographs of various types of boxes, vol. 1, pp. 125-240.

Anghiera, Pietro Martire. *De orbe novo decades*. First *Decade*, Seville, 1511; first complete edition (eight *Decades*), 1530. This work was the first to describe in any fulness the early voyages to America. The first English translation was by Richard Eden: the first three *Decades*, 1555; the complete work, 1577. The only probable reference to tobacco is in *Decade* III, book

8, where it is said: "There is also an herbe whose smoke is deadly poison."

Anonymous. *A Work for Chimney Sweepers, or a Warning to tobaconists, Describing the Pernicious Use of Tabaco* . . . London, 1602. The opening shot in the great English controversy over tobacco.

Arber, E. (Editor) English Reprints, James VI of Scotland, I of England. *The Essays of a Prentise in the Divine Art of Poesie, A Counterblaste to Tobacco.* London, 1869. The above contains documentary material relating to the early use of tobacco in France and England.

Bain, A. W. *Tobacco: Its History and Associations, Use and Abuse, including an Account of the Plant, and its Modes of Use in all Ages and Countries; showing it to be the Solace of the King and the Beggar; comprising Prints and Woodcuts; Portraits of renowned Smokers; Tobacco Papers; Numberless Cuttings and Extracts; Pipes, Cigars, Snuff and Snuff-Boxes, and all the Smoker's Paraphernalia; Statistics of Consumption, Revenue, etc., in relation to this Wonderful Weed, and in fact every con-*

ceivable item of interest that could be gathered in relation to the subject; the result of over thirty years' labor in collecting. 1836. Mounted and arranged in 17 large folio volumes; with specially printed title pages; bound in half green morocco extra, gilt tops. (Copied from Bragge, No. 228, page 39.)

Balde, Jakob. *Satyra contra abusum tabaci.* Monaco, 1657. Translated into German as *Die trockene Trunkenheit. . . . Satyra oder Straffrede wider den Missbrauch des Tabaka,* Nürnberg, 1658.

Bank, E. C. *Geschichte und Geschichten vom Tabak.* Leipzig, [1927].

Barclay, William. *Nepenthes, or the Vertues of Tobacco,* Edinburg, 1614.

Benzoni, Girolamo. *La historia del mondo nuovo.* Venetia, 1565. The result of fourteen years of exploration in the West Indies. Benzoni's work went through many editions and was translated into Latin and French.

Billings, E. R. *Tobacco: Its History, Varieties, Culture, Manufacture and Commerce, with an Account of its Various Modes of*

Use, from Its First Discovery Until Now —With Illustrations by Popular Artists. Hartford, Connecticut, 1875. A monograph of great interest and value.

Blondel, Spire. *Le tabac. Le livre des fumeurs et des priseurs.* Paris, 1891. Preface by Baron Oscar de Watteville; 16 coloured plates and other illustrations. It is interesting to note that *priser* means at once to take snuff and to set a high value on one's self.

Bouchot, Henry. *La miniature française, 1750-1825.* Paris, 1907. The standard French work with many fine illustrations. After Bouchot's death the above was revised by Frederick Masson as a handbook, 1910.

Bragge, William. *Bibliotheca Nicotiana; A Catalogue of Books about Tobacco, Together with a Catalogue of Objects Connected with the Use of Tobacco in All its Forms.* Second, greatly enlarged edition, privately printed, 200 copies. Birmingham, 1880. (My autographed copy is No. 163.) Bragge assembled the most complete collection of articles used in the consumption of tobacco that has ever been made by any one person or museum. In its dispersion foundations have been made for a great number and variety of special collections. The catalogue of articles in the snuff section, pages 179-248, include mills, rasps, jars, spoons, boxes, *netsukes,* and bottles. The descriptive catalogue of Chinese snuff-bottles is especially complete, covering thirty-five pages.

Brathwait, Richard. *The Smoking Age: or, The Man in a Mist, with the Life and Death of Tobacco.* London, 1617.

Brushfield, T. N. "Raleghana, Part II, The Introduction of the Potato and Tobacco into England and Ireland," *Report and Transactions of the Devonshire Association for the Advancement of Science, Literature and Art,* vol. XXX. Plymouth, 1898. (Tobacco, pp. 178-197.)

Buttes, Henry. *Dyets Dry Dinner.* London, 1599.

Cartier, Jacques, 1494-1552. Bref Récit et succincte narration de la Navigation faiteen 1535 et 1536 . . . aux iles de Canada, Hochelaga, Sagueney, et autres. Paris, 1545. Reprinted, edited by the Marquis d'Avezac, Paris, 1863. English translation by H. P. Biggar, *The Voyages of Jacques Cartier*, Ottawa, 1924. The *Brief récit* is the narrative in Cartier's second voyage, 1535, in which he tells of finding the Indians smoking tobacco along the St. Lawrence. The species was undoubtedly *Nicotiana rustica*, not *Nicotiana tabacum*, which was known only in Central and South America before the coming of the Europeans.

Columbus, Christopher. *Diario de la primera viaje*. First published by Martin Fernandez de Navarrete in his *Colección de los viajes y descubrimientos*, Madrid, 1825-37. The best English edition and translation is that by Cecil Jane, *The Voyages of Christopher Columbus*, London, 1930. Columbus's *Journal* for October 15 and November 6, 1492, contains the first references to tobacco by a European. See Las Casas.

Corti, Egon Cæsar, Conte. *Die trockene Trunkenheit; Ursprung, Kampf und Triumph des Rauchens*. Leipzig, 1930. 64 illustrations. Translated into English by Paul England as *A History of Smoking*,

London, 1931. Corti borrows his title from the German translation of a satire against tobacco by Jakob Balde (see Balde). The bibliography is extensive but defective, giving no light on the continuation of Schranka, and omitting any reference to the later (and infinitely more important) editions of Bragge and Fairhold. Although Corti's work is not critical, and is sometimes historically open to contradiction, it is the most recent and the most readable treatise on the history of smoking.

Curtis, E. S. *The North American Indian, Being a Series of Volumes Picturing and Describing the Indians of the United States, the Dominion of Canada, and Alaska.* Seattle, Wash., E. S. Curtis, and Cambridge, Mass., 1907-30. 20 volumes, folio, accompanied by 20 portfolios containing 1,000 full-page photogravures and 700 extra-sized plates printed in sepia. Edition limited to 500 sets. This is a truly monumental work in every way. The author hopes that it may be accepted as a partial atonement for the national disgrace involved in our treatment of the Indian.

Delamotte, W. A. (?) *Snuff and Snuff Takers: A Pungent, Piquant, Comical, Veritable and Historic Disquisition. To which is added A Dissertation on The Poetry of Sneezing.* London, 1846.

Denis, Jules. *Le tabac. Son histoire, sa production et sa consommation.* Genève, 1902.

Fairholt, F. W. (F.S.A.) *Tobacco: Its History and Associations. Including an Account of the Plant and Its Manufacture; with Its Modes of Use in All Ages and Countries.* London, 1859; second, greatly enlarged edition, London, 1876. With 100 illustrations by the author. Never using tobacco in any form, Fairholt assisted his father in a tobacco warehouse until his twenty-second year. His monograph, the result of many years' study, travel, and close observation is one of the best in any language.

Feinhals, Joseph. *Der Tabak in Kunst und Kultur.* Cöln, 1911.

Gumilla, Joseph. Historia Naturelle, civile et geographique de l'Orenoque. Avignon, 1758.

Harriot, Thomas. *A Briefe and True Report*

of the New Found Land of Virginia. . . . London, 1588. Reprinted, edited by L. S. Livingston, New York, 1903; facsimile. The first extended account of tobacco in England, apart from the translations of Thevet and Monardes. Harriot was in Virginia with Raleigh.

Harrison, William. *Great Chronologie.* Manuscript, preserved in three folio volumes in the Diocesan Library, Derry, Ireland. Extracts have been printed by F. J. Furnivall in his edition of Harrison's *Description of England*, London, The New Shakespeare Society, 1876. The entry for the year 1573, included among Furnivall's extracts, contains a discussion of tobacco. By virtue of this extract, Harrison becomes the first English author to use the word "tabaco," the first to record the custom of smoking in England, and the first to describe the remedial effects of the plant.

[Hill, Benson Earle] "Dean Snift of Brazen-Nose." *A Pinch—of Snuff: Composed of Curious Particulars and Original Anecdotes of Snuff-Taking; as well as a Review of Snuff, Snuff-Boxes, Snuff-Takers and*

Snuff-Papers; with the Moral and Physical Effects of Snuff. London, 1840. The preface is signed "Pollexenes Digit Snift, Dean of Brazen-Nose." There are six full-page plates by Thomas Sibson, as well as numerous lesser illustrations. Hill's book is amusing, interspersed with verses and anecdotes, but it is strictly a polite contribution to the literature of tobacco.

Hobson, R. L. *The Wares of the Ming Dynasty.* London, 1923. *The Later Ceramic Wares of China.* London, 1925. These sumptuous works of Hobson are supreme in their field, both as regards authority of text and beauty of illustration.

Hodge, F. W. *Handbook of American Indians.* Bureau of American Ethnology, Bulletin XXX. 2 vols., 1907. Reissued 1912, Washington.

Humboldt, Alexander von. *Un voyage aux régions équinoxiales du nouveau continent.* Paris, 1814-25. 9 vols.

James I. *A Counterblaste to Tobacco.* London, 1604. Often reprinted.

Las Casas, Bartolomé de. 1474-1566. *Historia de las Indias.* Written 1527-50. The

Mss. of Las Casas were long unknown but first published at Madrid, 1875-76, 6 vols., edited by the Marqués de la Fuensanta del Valle and J. Sancho Rayon. Corti erroneously states that the work is still in manuscript. We owe to Las Casas the preservation of considerable primary source-material concerning Columbus, including the invaluable *Journal* of the first voyage, as well as additional material which Las Casas incorporated into his history. See Columbus.

Laufer, Berthold. *The Introduction of Tobacco into Europe,* also *Tobacco and Its Use in Asia.* Chicago, Field Museum of Natural History, 1924. Anthropology leaflets. Interesting and suggestive.

Le Moyne, Jacques. *Brevis narratio eorum quae in Florida . . . acciderunt . . . anno MDLXIIII. . . .* Published by Theodor de Bry in his *Collections peregrinatioum,* Frankfurt, 1591.

Liebault, Jean. *L'agriculture et maison rustique,* sixth edition. Paris, 1570. This work often erroneously referred to the brothers Liebault and less often to Charles

Etienne or Estienne and Jean Liebault, was originally the work of Estienne who died before its publication. This was carried on by his son-in-law Jean Liebault, who added much as the work went through twenty editions before 1600 and was translated into the chief languages of Europe. The Nicot chapter probably appeared first in the sixth edition which was the one from which Frampton made his translation and which fixed the technical term *Nicotiana* on tobacco.

L'Obel, Matthias, and Pena, Petrus. *Stirpium adversaria nova. . . .* London, 1570. This work states that tobacco was then being grown in England. Plantarum sev Stirpium Historia, Antwerp, 1576. L'Obel (Lobel, Lobelius) was later chief botanist to James I.

Machen, Arthur (?). *Tobacco Talk and Smokers' Gossip; an Amusing Miscellany of Fact and Anecdote Relating to the "Great Plant" in All Its Forms and Uses, Including a Selection from Nicotian Literature.* London, 1886.

MacInnes, C. M. *The Early English Tobacco*

Trade. London, 1926. An excellent survey.

McGuire, J. D. *Pipes and Smoking Customs of the American Aborigines.* Washington, D. C., 1899; Report of U. S. National Museum, 1897, pp. 351-645. 239 illustrations, plate, 4 maps. McGuire is in error as to pipes in South America. (See Stahl.)

Meller, H. J. *Nicotiana, or the Smoker's and Snuff Taker's Companion, Containing the History of Tobacco with an Essay in its Defence.* London, 1832.

Mocq, Henry, and Dreyfus, Carl. *Tabatières, boîtes et étuis.* Paris, 1930. Chiefly devoted to illustrations of snuff-boxes, with descriptions.

Monardes, Nicolás. *Primera y segunda y tercera partes de la historia medicinal de las Cosas que se traen de nuestras Indias Occidentales, que sirven en medicina. . . .* Sevilla, 1574. Translated by John Frampton as *Joyfull Newes out of the Newe Founde Worlde,* London, 1577; second edition, 1580; reprinted with an introduction by Stephen Gaselee, London and New York, 1925, 2 vols., 1,025 copies. The Spanish edition published in 1574 includes two earlier works of Monardes, 1569-1571, which had become very popular. Monardes did more than any one else to propagate a belief in the sovereign properties of tobacco as a panacea. His work was translated into all the leading languages of Europe. Frampton's version, which includes a section translated from the *Agriculture* of Liebault, contains the second *printed* reference to tobacco in English (*cf.* Sparke, Thevet, and Harrison), and introduced the union of Nicot and Nicotiana to the English-speaking world.

Nadaillac, Jean François Albert du Pouget, Marquis de. *Les pipes et le tabac.* Paris, 1885.

Neander, Johann, of Bremen. *Tabacologia: hoc est, tabaci, sen Nicotianae descriptio Medico — Cheirurgico — Pharmaceutica; &c.* Leyden, Isaac Elzevir, 1626. The earliest attempt at a comprehensive treatise.

Oppel, Alwin. *Der Tabak in dem Wirtschaftsleben und der Sittengeschichte der Volker.* Bremen, 1890.

Oviedo y Valdes, Gonzalo Fernandez de. *Su-*

mario de la natural y general istoria de las Indias. Madrid, 1526. Enlarged edition, 1535-57; reprinted, edited by J. Amador de los Rios, Madrid, 1851-55, 4 vols. Oviedo's history is next after that of Peter Martyr in point of time, preceding Las Casas, Gómara Diaz, and all the Portuguese. Oviedo himself is commonly credited with the introduction of tobacco into Europe, 1519, and his book contains one of the first clear descriptions of the plant.

Pane, Ramón. *De insularium ritibus.* Written 1497. First published in the *Historie del S.D.F.C., nelle quali s'he particolare et vera relatione della vita et de' fatti dell' Ammiraglio Cristoforo Colombo*, Venice, 1571, an Italian translation by S. A. Ulloa of Ferdinand Columbus's life of his father. Pane's account, following close upon the allusions of Columbus, stands as the first definite discussion of tobacco, though it is not nearly so full as Oviedo's.

Parisiene, Jacques Gohorry. *Instruction sur l'herbe Petun ditte eu France l'Herbe de la Royne, ou Medicee.* Paris, 1572.

Partington, Wilfred. *Smoke Rings and Roun-*

delays, Blendings from Prose and Verse since Raleigh's Time. London, 1924; New York, 1925.

Penn, W. A. *The Soverane Herbe; a History of Tobacco.* London, Grant Richards, 1901. Includes an intelligent discussion of snuff.

Pilz, Hermann. *Uber den Tabak und des Rauchen; Ernestes und Heiteres aue der Culturgeschichte.* Leipzig, 1899.

Roger-Miles, L. *Comment Discerner les Styles du VIII au XIX Siecle.* A practical study of forms and decorations with seventeen hundred reproductions. Paris, n.d. It was published under the patronage of the minister of public instruction, and of the Beaux-Arts. This edition *de luxe* was later, 1909, published in three volumes.

Shranka, Eduard Maria. *Tabakanecdoten; ein historisches Braunbuch aus den verschiedensten Quellen zusammengetragen und nach den Personlichkeiten alphabetisch geordnet.* . . . Cöln, 1914. 175 illustrations.

Sebillot, Paul. *Le tabac dans les traditions, les superstitions et les coutumes.* Paris, 1893.

BIBLIOGRAPHY

Singer, Charles. "The Early History of Tobacco," in *The Quarterly Review*, No. 436 (July, 1913). An excellent survey, with a judicious account of Thevet.

Snuff-Tubes. Uhle, Dr. Max, "A Snuffing-Tube from Tiahuanaco," *Bulletin, Philadelphia Free Museum of Science and Art*. I., 1898, pp. 159-177. Illus. Safford, William E., "Identity of Cohoba, the Narcotic Snuff of Ancient Haiti." J. Wash. Acad. Sci., 6, pp. 547-562 (1916). Latcham, Ricardo E., "Tubes para aspirar Rapé, condecoracion Centro Americano," *Revista Chilena de Historia Natural*, XXXI (1927), pp. 252-255. Illus.

Sparke, John. Acount of Hawkins's Second Voyage, 1564-65. Probably written 1565. First published in Hakluyt's *The Principall Navigations, Voiages and Discoveries of the English Nation*, London, 1589; standard edition, Glasgow, J. MacLehose and Sons, 1903-05, 12 vols. Sparke's mention of tobacco is the earliest in English, as far as is known, but it was not published until twenty-one years after the appearance of the anonymous translation of Thevet.

Spenser, Edmund. *The Faerie Queene.* London, 1590. Book III, canto v, stanza 32, contains the first reference to tobacco to be found in English poetry.

Stahl, Gunther. "Der Tabak im Leben Südamerikanischer Völker," *Zeitschrift für Ethnologie,* LVII (1925), pp. 81-152 Ill., maps; bibliography. A very technical review of the field, showing the presence of all modes of tobacco consumption, and that pipes in pre-Columbian times in South America were more widely used than is generally supposed.

Stalker, John. *A Treatise of Japanning and Varnishing, being a compleat Discovery of those Arts. With the best way of making all sorts of Varnish for Japan, Wood, Prints, or Pictures. The Method of Guilding, Burnishing, and Lackering, with the Art of Guilding, Separating, and Refining Metals, and of Painting Mezzo-tinto Prints. Also Rules for Counterfeiting Tortoise-shell, and Marble, and for Staining or Dying Wood, Ivory, and Horn. Together with above an Hundred distinct Patterns for Japan-work, in imitation of the Indians, for*

Tables, Stands, Frames, Cabinets, Boxes, &c. Oxford, 1688. Folio, with 24 copper plates of designs for Powder Boxes, etc., etc.

Sylvester, Joshua. *Tobacco Battered, and the Pipes Shattered (About Their Eares that Idley Idolise so Base and Barbarous a Weed; or at least-wise Over-love so Loathsome Vanitie): by a Volley of Holy Shot Thundered from Mount Helicon. . . .* London, 1614.

Teall, Gardner. "The Treasured Snuff Bottles of the Celestials," in *House and Garden*, XXXIII, 3 (March, 1918, 26-27-28).

Thevet, André. *Les Singvlaritéz de la France antarctiqve, avtrement nommée Amériqve.* . . . Antwerp and Paris, 1558. Anonymously (Edward Place ?) translated into English as *The New Founde Worlde, or Antarcticke*, London, 1568. Thevet brought tobacco *tabacum* with him from Brazil and planted it in the neighbourhood of his native town of Angoulême some years before Nicot "introduced" tobacco *rustica* into France from Portugal. The English translation of *Les Singularitéz* has the distinction of containing the first *printed* account of tobacco in English (*cf.* Sparke, Harrison, and Monardes). Thevet also published *La cosmographie universelle*. Paris, 1575; 2 vols. In this later work, Thevet says: "I am the first who brought tobacco to France and planted it there and called it the herb of Angoulême. Since then a certain man who has never been in America has chosen to give it his own name." On Thevet see also Singer and Paul Gaffarel's *Notice Biographique* prefixed to his reprint of the Singularitéz, Paris, 1878.

Tiedemann, Friedrich. *Geschichte des Tabaks und anderer anlicher Genussmittel.* Frankfurt, 1854.

Westminster Tobacco Box. The first description of this box was printed and published by I. Clark, 27 Dartmouth Street, Westminster, in 1824, bearing the title: *Representations of the Embossed, Chased, & Engraved Subjects and Inscriptions which Decorate the Tobacco Box and Cases, Belonging to the Past Overseers' Society of the Parishes of St. Margaret and St. John*

the Evangelist in the City of Westminster.
The above is reproduced in *Chats on Old English Tobacco Jars* by Reginald Myer, London and Philadelphia, no date, but probably about 1930, and in Smith, J. E., *The Westminster Box*, London, Westminster, 1887.

Wiener, Leo. *Africa and the Discovery of America.* Philadelphia, 1920-22, three volumes, and a supplement, *The Philological History of "Tobacco" in America*, Goteborg, 1925. Professor Wiener presents the astonishing theses that the early explorers of the New World nowhere found tobacco in use, and that tobacco was not native to America but was introduced from Africa by negro slaves. This type of historical method is aptly described by MacInnes as "an attempt to discredit undoubted descriptions of early writers, and, where this cannot be done, to ignore or misrepresent them."

SOME EIGHTEENTH CENTURY DEALERS IN SNUFF BOXES

THERE were a number of jewellers in the eighteenth century who dealt very extensively in snuff boxes. Among them the better known—as miniaturists or makers—are the Petitots (father and son); Jean Ducrolloy, Pierre Joseph Antoine, Jean Moynat, the Sagarets, Jean George and Charles Banabé, Pierre Jean Bellangé, Mathieu Coiny, Louis François Auguste Taunay, Étienne Bleizy, Pierre Jean Leufant, Barthelémy Pittieu, Maximilian Vachette, Barbe, Daniel Chodowiecki of Dantzig, Neuber of Dresden.

Courtesy of Harriet Johnson

PART TWO
LIST OF ILLUSTRATIONS

LIST OF ILLUSTRATIONS

(15) CURIOSO.
    a. Papier Mâché. Verni Martin shoe snuff box. Double. With portraits of two of Napoleon's Marshals. "Vive les chasseurs de la Garde."
    b. Boxwood snuff box. Mermaid. Double covers. Crude. Spanish.
    c. Olive wood snuff box. Monk, ivory buttons and eyes. Spanish.
    d. Red hardwood. Beautifully carved shoe with two sliding covers. 18th century.

(16) SNUFF BOX. Thunga wood with tortoise shell bands. Painting of woman holding cherries. The cover glass mounted in gold band.

(17) SNUFF BOX. Thunga wood. Top enriched with painting of two figures in gay colors. Falstaff and maid. Signed E. Duchez.

(18) CLASSICAL. TORTOISE SHELL SNUFF BOX. With gold bands. Glow of sunset over a delicate landscape.

(19) TORTOISE SHELL SNUFF BOX. Angel and kneeling woman.

(20) THUNGA WOOD AND IVORY SNUFF BOX. A young man and woman standing before a statue of Cupid.

(21) THUNGA WOOD SNUFF BOX. Verni Martin. Beautiful landscape with four figures.

(22) ROUND THUNGA WOOD SNUFF BOX. "Henry Quatre le bien Aimé." Tout perissait enfin lorsque Bourbon parut. French.

(23) THUNGA WOOD SNUFF BOX. (Rare.) Cranologie du Docteur Gall. Reverse side "Systeme des organes Cerebreaux de Doc't Gall.

(24) PAPIER-MÂCHÉ SNUFF BOX. Verni Martin. Dr. Faustus. 1525. Auerback's Keller, (top). Banquet scene, (bottom).

(25) PAPIER-MÂCHÉ SNUFF BOX. Verni Martin. Napoleon Hat. 1798.

(26) SILVER SNUFF BOX. Verni Martin. Le Sage—Gil Blas. Book form.

(27) PAPIER-MÂCHÉ SNUFF BOX. Sailing ships, one flying Union Jack. Military flag and Admiral of the fleet.

ILLUSTRATIONS

(28) Wood. Polysander Near Rosewood Snuff Box. Bands and design of silver. "Man and oxen ploughing."

(29) Copper, Bronze and Silver Snuff Box. Repoussé. Top several figures.

(30) Metal Veneered Snuff Box. Inlaid with gold. Oval bloodstone in center.

(31*a*) Chinese Snuff Bottle. Cylindrical. Coral top. Four Mandarin figures in blue. Kang Hsi period. 1622-1723.

(31*b*) Chinese Snuff Bottle. Cylindrical. Silver top. Red dragon encircling bottle. Other marks in blue. 1662-1723.

(31*c*) Chinese Snuff Bottle. Cylindrical. Egg shell crackle. Blue dragon encircling bottle. Gold stone top. Yung Chang period. 250 years old.

(32*a*) Chinese Patendre Snuff Bottle. In grey, brown, lavender and light blue. Fifteen human figures in cameo. Elaborate inscription on bottom. Pink bronze stopper.

(32*b*) Chinese Snuff Bottle. Pink porcelain with black symbols. Jade top. (New silver band.) Ming Dynasty, 1522-50.

(32*c*) Porcelain Snuff Bottle. Figures on both sides in Medallion. Framed in blue.

(32*d*) Porcelain Snuff Bottle. Slightly grey. Figure and tree dark blue. These two bottles (*c* and *d*) found in effects of an old missionary to China. 1860-1880.

(33*a*) Chinese Snuff Bottle. Clear glass overlaid with dark red dragons. Green jade top.

(33*b*) Chinese Snuff Bottle. Twelve animal figures in blue on bluish white. Amber and silver top. 17th century.

(33*c*) Chinese Snuff Bottle. Red symbols on grey glass. "Double fish double happiness" in all 8 symbols. Coral and jade stopper.

(33*d*) Opaque Mottled White Glass Snuff Bottle. Overlaid with red glass flowers. Flat Calabash shape.

(34) Four Chinese Snuff Bottles with Inner Paintings. *a.* Crystal. Coral and gold top. Several figures and inscription.

[143]

b. Brown glass. Rich in color. Six figures. Inscription. Coral top.

c. Glass. (Modern.) With several figures. Moonstone stopper.

d. Glass. Painted on four sides and bottom. Seven figures, birds, flowers and lettering.

(35) GOLD SNUFF BOX. Engraved on all sides. Shield on top contains ivory miniature of Mme. Roland by François Dumont (?). French.

(36) JEAN PETITOT. 1607-1691. Miniature of Le Duc d'Ollone of Louis XIV fame. Done in enamel. Placed later on gold enamel, 18th century oval snuff box. Done chiefly in gold starred translucent green surrounded by white enamel bands and pink stones.

(37) IVORY POLYCHROME SNUFF BOTTLE. Imperial of 17th century. Carved on both sides. Horse and rider and other figures. Signature on bottom.

(38) IVORY SNUFF BOTTLE. Beautifully decorated in black, white and red. Lacquered. Imperial bottle. Chien Lung. 1736-1795.

(39) IVORY SNUFF BOTTLE. Shape of Egyptian vase or mummy. Carved on both sides.

(40) AMBER SNUFF BOTTLE. Carved with horse and human figures. Chinese stamp on bottom. Coral top.

(41) SNUFF GRATER FORMED OF A SHELL OF THE TROPICAL STAG COWRY. Mounted in silver. English. Early 18th century. (Victoria and Albert Museum.)

(42) SNUFF GRATER OF SILVER. Engraved with the crest of Edmonds (Yorkshire) and monogram of H. E. English. About 1700. (Victoria and Albert Museum.)

(43) SNUFF GRATER OF SILVER. Cylindrical. Two hinges. Exquisite workmanship. (George III.)

(44) SNUFF SPOON. Silver. Queen Anne. 1702-14.

(45) STOBWASSER BOXES.

    a. Papier-Mâché snuff box. Woman reclining on couch holding bunch of grapes. Beautiful in color and modeling.

    b. Papier-Mâché snuff box. Portrait of Clarissa Harlowe. Name inside the lid.

ILLUSTRATIONS

c. Papier-Mâché snuff box. Portrait of a lady. "Bonjour" inside the lid. 18th century.

(46) SCOTCH MULL. Polished horn with repoussé silver top. Light cairngorm stone. Silver ball and tongue hinge. Duke of Sutherland's collection with crest.

(47) SCOTCH MULL. Polished horn. Silver mountings. Dark cairngorm stone. Inscribed "John Graeme."

(48*a*) SCOTCH MULL. Dark horn. Mounted in silver. Agate insert.

(48*b*) SCOTCH MULL. Dark horn. Bound in silver. Silver hinge. Marked W.P.B.

(49) GOLD SNUFF BOX. Richly engraved. Set with diamonds. Early XIX century. Russian. (Courtesy of Cleveland Museum of Art.)

(50) GOLD SNUFF BOX. White enamel lines. Three figures. French. Louis XVI period. (Courtesy of Cleveland Museum of Art.)

(51) DARK ENAMEL AND GOLD SNUFF BOX. Diamond shape with landscape. Castle of Chillon. Swiss or French. (Courtesy of Cleveland Museum of Art.)

(52) GOLD AND ENAMEL SNUFF BOX SET WITH DIAMONDS. Inside of lid ivory miniature of Frederick the Great. Maker probably Daniel Bandisson. German. 1765-1775. (Courtesy of The Metropolitan Museum of Art.)

(53) GOLD AND ENAMEL SNUFF BOX. Oval. Rococo ornament. Battle scene. Middle 18th century. Germany? (Courtesy of The Metropolitan Museum of Art.)

(54) HELIOTROPE SNUFF BOX. Mounted in gold. Set with emerald and diamonds. Formerly in the Galitzine collection. First half 18th century. (Courtesy of The Metropolitan Museum of Art.)

(55) SNUFF BOTTLE. Amber. Chien Lung Period. 1736-1795. (Courtesy of Metropolitan Museum of Art.)

(56) WHITE PORCELAIN SNUFF BOTTLE IN OPEN WORK DESIGN. Modern. Red glass stopper. (Courtesy of The Metropolitan Museum of Art.)

(57) SNUFF BOTTLE. Twin. Porcelain. Decorated with famille rose enamel. Chien Lung period. 1736-1795. (Courtesy of The Metropolitan Museum of Art.)

[145]

(58) LAVENDER AND GREEN SNUFF BOTTLE. Jadeite. Chien Lung. 1736-1795. (Courtesy of The Metropolitan Museum of Art.)

(59) SNUFF BOX. Firegilt. Oval. Chased in diaper pattern. Enamel miniature. "Fabiola" after Henner. French.

(60) FIREGILT SNUFF BOX. Round, heavy repoussé at sides. Miniature on ivory. Signed "Hermandez." French.

(61) FIREGILT SNUFF BOX. Chased with diaper pattern. Painting on ivory. "Fishing Party." Signed. A. de St. Marc. French.

(62) IVORY SNUFF BOX. Round. Miniature on ivory set in gold. French.

(63) ECCLESIASTICAL ROUND BOX-WOOD SNUFF BOX. Beautifully carved. Screw top with inner metal clasp. "Christus."

(64) REVERSE SIDE, "Mary."

(65) PAPIER-MÂCHÉ SNUFF BOX. Black with cameo insert of Pope Pius IX. 1870.

(66) DARK WOOD SNUFF BOX. Silver ends. Silver Monstrance on ivory cover. Clasp in silver. Marked, "Victoria B. F." Italian.

(67) COPPER SNUFF BOX. Verni Martin. Oval. Painting after "Boucher."

(68) DARK TORTOISE SHELL SNUFF BOX. Fluted. Gold hinges and gold stars inset.

(69) SNUFF BOXES MADE OF INDIAN BETEL NUT. Dark brown. Deeply carved on both sides. One with figures, the other with symbols and flowers.

(70a) DARK BLUE COMPOSITION SNUFF BOX. Gilt bronze portrait of Voltaire.

(70b) WOOD SNUFF BOX. Medallion in silver. "Ceres."

(70c) WOOD SNUFF BOX. General Washington. Medallion in gold. Under glass. Circa 1778.

(70d) MOTTLED WOOD SNUFF BOX. Medallion in copper of Luther, Churf and Melanchthon. Dated 1830. Memorial.

(70e) NAPOLEON AND LOUISE.

[146]

ILLUSTRATIONS

(71) TIN SNUFF BOX. Verni Martin finish. Richly colored. Ballet dancer.

(72) PEWTER SNUFF BOX. Motto, "Sic Publico Commoda Stabunt."

(73) BRASS AND BRONZE SNUFF BOX. "England expects every man to do his duty." Admiral Nelson. Trafalgar. Oct. XXI, MDCCCV.

(74) APPLE WOOD SNUFF BOX. With five lids. Dog in mother of pearl on bright red ground.

(75) BLACK BONE SNUFF BOX. Adam and Eve. The tree and the serpent. "Le fruit defendu."

(76) OVAL BRASS SNUFF BOX. With silver lid and hinge bottom. Floral engraving. "Chiolerio Cio Francesco." 1856.

(77) BRONZE OCTAGONAL SNUFF BOX. Head of Gustavus Adolphus. Bottom, coat of arms.

(78) BRASS AND MOTHER OF PEARL HEART SHAPED SNUFF BOX.

(79) WROUGHT IRON SNUFF BOX. Very rare. Finely done in vines and flowers. Gold background. Given by a German Prince to Bishop —— of Washington, D. C.

(80) EARLY 19TH CENTURY TIN SNUFF BOX. Said to be portrait of Jenny Lind. Fashion of 1830.

(81) TORTOISE SHELL SNUFF BOX. Portrait on ivory Louis XVIII with decoration. French.

(82) TORTOISE SHELL SNUFF BOX WITH GILT BANDS. Miniature in ivory. Gentleman with stock. Early 19th century.

(83) MOTTLED TORTOISE SHELL SNUFF BOX. Miniature on ivory. Young student. Light blue background. Gold band.

(84) PAPIER-MÂCHÉ SNUFF BOX. Copy Romney's portrait of "Cowper."

(85) PAPIER-MÂCHÉ SNUFF BOX. Verni Martin. Picture of St. Peter. Done in rich browns.

(86) PAPIER-MÂCHÉ SNUFF BOX. Table box. Old man with red cap trimmed with fur. Brown cloak.

(87) PAPIER-MÂCHÉ SNUFF BOX. Old bearded man with red cloak. 18th century.

(88) PAPIER-MÂCHÉ SNUFF BOX. "The Dentist Shop." After Teniers.

(89) PAPIER-MÂCHÉ SNUFF BOX. Master with pipe. Servant bringing beer.

(90) PAPIER-MÂCHÉ SNUFF BOX. Gaily painted hunting scene. Lines painted in gold.

(91*a*) BONE SNUFF BOX. Two finger opening. Book form. Hot needle engraving. 1847. Spanish.

(91*b*) BONE SNUFF BOX. Oval with hot needle engraving; lettering in German.

(91*c*) HORN SNUFF BOX. Brass bound ends. Top ivory with hot point drawing of flowers.

(92) PAPIER-MÂCHÉ SNUFF BOX. King Henry of Navarre in action.

(93) HEAVY TORTOISE SHELL SNUFF BOX. Bound in silver with silver hinges. Fine example of piqué gold work.

(94) WOOD SNUFF BOX. Bound in brass. Mosaic top. Made of fish scales in colors. Soldiers fighting.

(95) BLONDE TORTOISE SHELL SNUFF BOX. Inlaid with gold. Balloon ascension. Circa 1783.

(96) TURQUOISE ENCASED IN SILVER WITH SILVER TOP AND SPOON. Turquoise insets.

(97) CHINESE SNUFF BOTTLES. Silver with silver top and spoons. Formerly medicine bottles.

(98*a*) DARK TORTOISE SHELL SNUFF BOX. Deeply carved (top).

(98*b*) SAME. (Bottom.) Chinese.

(99) PORCELAIN SNUFF BOX. Mounted in gold. Profile portrait of Washington. Flanked by sprays of oak leaves. Gilt on a white ground. Germany. (Meissen.) 1814-1818. (Courtesy of the Metropolitan Museum of Art.)

(100) IVORY AND GOLD SNUFF BOX. Tortoise shell lining. Profile portrait of Franklin in stipple engraving on paper. English. Late 18th or early 19th century. (Courtesy of the Metropolitan Museum of Art.)

(101) TORTOISE SHELL AND GOLD SNUFF BOX. Portrait of Lafayette painted in grisaille on a white porcelain plaque. Probably French. Late 18th century. (Courtesy of the Metropolitan Museum of Art.)

ILLUSTRATIONS

NOTE

All unattributed articles illustrated are from the author's collection.

FIG. 2. CHINESE SNUFF
BOTTLE

Yunanjade. Dark emerald
green. Flowers and birds
carved in high relief in
scrolls.

FIG. 3. CHINESE SNUFF BOTTLE

Jadeite. Moss green. Finely
carved. Coral top on metal.

FIG. 4. CHINESE SNUFF
BOTTLE

Rosequartz. Light pink.
Tree pattern in high re-
lief.

FIG. 5. CHINESE SNUFF BOTTLE

Agate. Grey and black. Carved
white figures of animals. Carnelian stopper.

FIG. 6.   SÈVRES.   TWO COMPARTMENT SNUFF BOX
Delicate pink.   Painted on all sides.

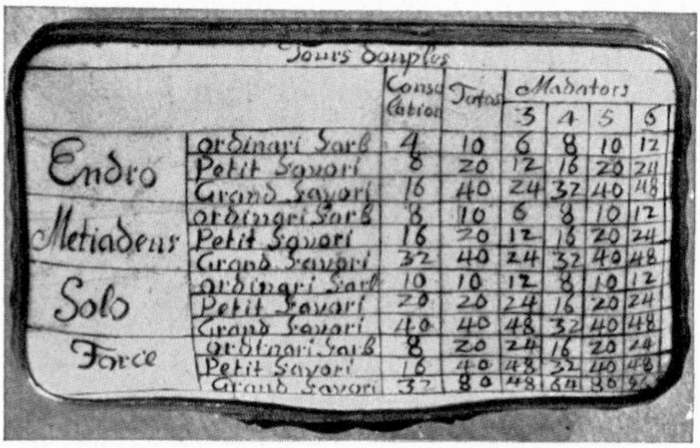

FIG. 7.   WHITE ENAMEL SPORTING SNUFF BOX
Playing cards on each side.   Bull fight score
top and bottom.

FIG. 8.   BATTERSEA.   ENAMEL SNUFF BOX
With ships and portrait of Admiral Nelson inside the lid.   18th century.

FIG. 9. CHINESE JADE SNUFF BOX
Deeply carved and set in gilt.

FIG. 10. ROUND COMBINATION SNUFF AND PATCH
BOX

Two lids. Alternate panels firegilt repoussé and
composition. Yellow and brown.

FIG. 11. FIREGILT SNUFF BOX
Engraved. On enamel center two cupids. Lapis lazuli corners.

FIG. 12. SNUFF BOX. DEEPLY CARVED IVORY TOP
Bound in silver. Louis XV period.

FIG. 13. SNUFF BOX. "SACRA FAMILIA"

Carved mother of pearl. Octagonal. Bound and
clamped in silver. Three figures in relief.

FIG. 14. SNUFF BOX. CAPO DI MONTE

Evidently old (i.e. before 1759). Unmarked. Decorated in delicate flesh tones and colors on white
background. Venus and three cupids. Bound and
lined with gilt.

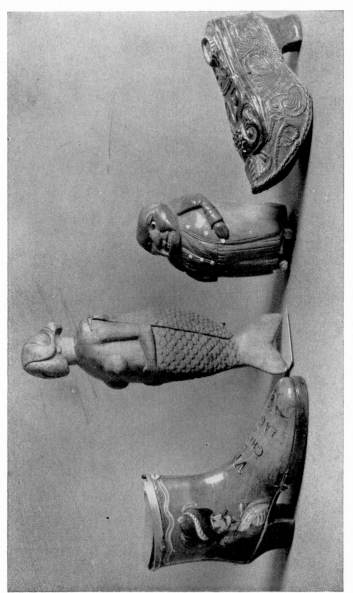

Fig. 15. Curioso

a. Papier-Mâché. Verni Martin shoe snuff box. Double. With portraits of two of Napoleon's Marshals. "Vive les chausseurs de la Garde." *b*. Boxwood snuff box. Mermaid. Double covers. Crude. Spanish. *c*. Olive wood snuff box. Monk, ivory buttons and eyes. Spanish. *d*. Red hardwood. Beautifully carved shoe with two sliding covers. 18th century.

FIG. 16. SNUFF BOX

Thunga wood with tortoise shell bands. Painting of woman
holding cherries. The cover glass mounted in gold band.

FIG. 17. SNUFF BOX

Thunga wood. Top enriched with painting of
two figures in gay colors. Falstaff and maid.
Signed E. Duchez.

Classical

FIG. 18. TORTOISE SHELL SNUFF BOX

With gold bands. Glow of sunset over a delicate landscape.

FIG. 19. TORTOISE SHELL SNUFF BOX

Angel and kneeling woman.

FIG. 20.   THUNGA WOOD AND IVORY SNUFF BOX

A young man and woman standing before a statue
of Cupid.

FIG. 21.   THUNGA WOOD SNUFF BOX

Verni Martin.   Beautiful landscape with four
figures.

FIG. 22. ROUND THUNGA WOOD SNUFF BOX

"Henry Quatre le bien Aimé." Tout perissait enfin
lorsque Bourbon parut. French.

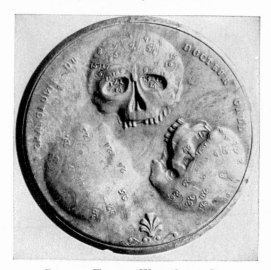

FIG. 23. THUNGA WOOD SNUFF BOX

(Rare.) Cranologie du Docteur Gall. Reverse
side "Systeme des organes Cerebreaux de Doc't
Gall."

FIG. 24. PAPIER-MÂCHÉ SNUFF BOX
Verni Martin. Dr. Faustus. 1525. Auerbach's Keller
(top). Banquet scene (bottom).

Fig. 25 (upper left). Papier-Mâché Snuff Box. Verni Martin.
Napoleon Hat. 1798. Fig. 26 (upper right). Silver Snuff Box. Verni Martin.
Le Sage—Gil Blas. Book form. Fig. 27 (left centre). Papier-Mâché Snuff
Box. Sailing ships, one flying Union Jack. Military flag and Admiral of the
fleet. Fig. 28 (right centre). Wood. Polysander near-rosewood snuff box.
Bands and design of silver. "Man and oxen ploughing." Fig. 29 (lower left).
Copper, bronze and silver snuff box. Repoussé. Top several figures. Fig. 30
(lower right). Metal veneered snuff box. Inlaid with gold. Oval bloodstone
in centre.

FIG. 31a. CHINESE SNUFF BOTTLE. Cylindrical. Coral top. Four Mandarin figures in blue. Kang Hsi period. 1662-1723. FIG. 31b. CHINESE SNUFF BOTTLE. Cylindrical. Silver top. Red dragon encircling bottle. Other marks in blue. 1662-1723. FIG. 31c. CHINESE SNUFF BOTTLE. Cylindrical. Egg shell crackle. Blue dragon encircling bottle. Gold stone top. Yung Chang period. 250 years old.

FIG. 32a. CHINESE PATENDRE SNUFF BOTTLE. In grey, brown, lavender, and light blue. Fifteen human figures in cameo. Elaborate
inscription on bottom. Pink bronze stopper. FIG. 32b. CHINESE
SNUFF BOTTLE. Pink porcelain with black symbols. Jade top. (New
silver band.) Ming Dynasty, 1522-50. FIG. 32c. PORCELAIN SNUFF
BOTTLE. Figures on both sides in Medallion. Framed in blue.
FIG. 32d. PORCELAIN SNUFF BOTTLE. Slightly grey. Figure and tree
dark blue. These two bottles (c and d) found in effects of an old
missionary to China. 1860-1880.

Fig. 33a. CHINESE SNUFF BOTTLE. Clear glass overlaid with dark red dragons. Green jade top. Fig. 33b. CHINESE SNUFF BOTTLE. Twelve animal figures in blue on bluish white. Amber and silver top. 17th century. Fig. 33c. CHINESE SNUFF BOTTLE. Red symbols on grey glass. "Double fish double happiness" in all 8 symbols. Coral and jade stopper. Fig. 33d. OPAQUE MOTTLED WHITE GLASS SNUFF BOTTLE. Overlaid with red glass flowers. Flat calabash shape.

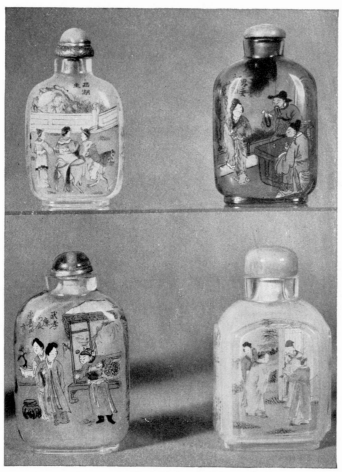

FIG. 34. FOUR CHINESE SNUFF BOTTLES WITH INNER PAINTINGS

a. Crystal. Coral and gold top. Several figures and inscription.
b. Brown glass. Rich in color. Six figures. Inscription. Coral top.
c. Glass. (Modern.) With several figures. Moonstone stopper.
d. Glass. Painted on four sides and bottom. Seven figures, birds,
flowers and lettering.

FIG. 35. GOLD SNUFF BOX

Engraved on all sides. Shield on top contains ivory miniature of Mme. Roland by François Dumont (?).

FIG. 36. JEAN PETITOT. 1607-1691.

Miniature of Le Duc d'Ollone of Louis XIV fame. Done
in enamel. Placed later on gold enamel. 18th century
oval snuff box. Done chiefly in gold starred translucent
green surrounded by white enamel bands and pink stones.

FIG. 37. IVORY POLYCHROME SNUFF
BOTTLE

Imperial of 17th century. Carved on
both sides. Horse and rider and other
figures. Signature on bottom.

FIG. 38. IVORY SNUFF BOTTLE

Beautifully decorated in black, white
and red. Lacquered. Imperial bottle. Chien Lung. 1736-1795.

FIG. 39. IVORY SNUFF BOTTLE

Shape of Egyptian vase or
mummy. Carved on both sides.

FIG. 40. AMBER SNUFF BOTTLE

Carved with horse and human figures.
Chinese stamp on bottom. Coral top.

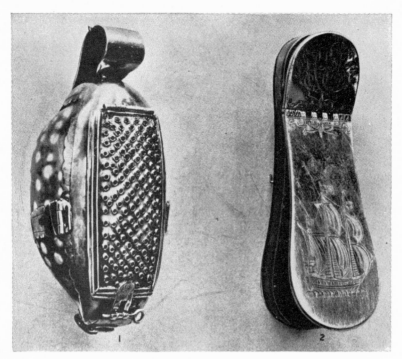

SNUFF GRATERS

FIG. 41 (1). Snuff grater formed of a shell of the tropical stag cowry. Mounted in silver. English. Early 18th century. (Victoria and Albert Museum.)

FIG. 42 (2). Snuff grater of silver. Engraved with the crest of Edmonds (Yorkshire) and monogram of H. E. English. About 1700. (Victoria and Albert Museum.)

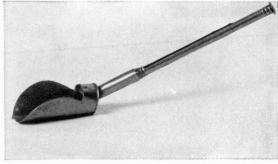

FIG. 43. SNUFF GRATER OF SILVER

Cylindrical. Two hinges. Exquisite workmanship. (George III.)

FIG. 44. SNUFF SPOON

Silver. Queen Anne. 1702-14.

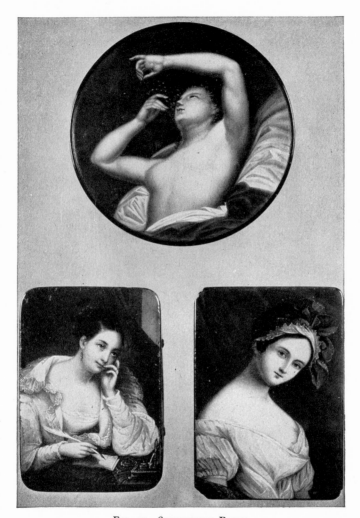

FIG. 45. STOBWASSER BOXES

a. Papier-Mâché snuff box. Woman reclining on couch holding
bunch of grapes. Beautiful in color and modeling. *b*. Papier-
Mâché snuff box. Portrait of Clarissa Harlowe. Name inside the
lid. *c*. Papier-Mâché snuff box. Portrait of a Lady. "Bonjour"
inside the lid. 18th century.

FIG. 46. SCOTCH MULL

Polished horn with repoussé silver top. Light
cairngorm stone. Silver ball and tongue hinge.
Duke of Sutherland's collection with crest.

FIG. 47. SCOTCH MULL

Polished horn. Silver mountings. Dark
cairngorm stone. Inscribed "John
Graeme."

FIG. 48*a*. SCOTCH MULL
Dark horn. Mounted in silver. Agate insert.

FIG. 48*b*. SCOTCH MULL
Dark horn. Bound in silver. Silver hinge.
Marked W.P.B.

FIG. 49. GOLD SNUFF BOX

Richly engraved. Set with diamonds. Early XIX century. Russian.

Courtesy of Cleveland Museum of Art

FIG. 50. GOLD SNUFF BOX

White enamel lines. Three figures. French. Louis XVI period.

Courtesy of Cleveland Museum of Art

FIG. 51. DARK ENAMEL AND GOLD SNUFF BOX
Diamond shape with landscape. Castle of Chillon. Swiss or French.
Courtesy of Cleveland Museum of Art

FIG. 52. GOLD AND ENAMEL SNUFF BOX SET WITH DIAMONDS
Inside of lid ivory miniature of Frederick the Great. Maker probably
Daniel Bandisson. German. 1765-1775.
Courtesy of the Metropolitan Museum of Art

FIG. 53. GOLD AND ENAMEL SNUFF BOX

Oval. Rococo ornament. Battle scene. Middle 18th century.
Germany?

Courtesy of the Metropolitan Museum of Art

FIG. 54. HELIOTROPE SNUFF BOX

Mounted in gold. Set with emerald and diamonds.
Formerly in the Galitzine collection. First half 18th century.

Courtesy of the Metropolitan Museum of Art

FIG. 55. SNUFF BOTTLE
Amber.   Chien Lung Period.   1736-1795.
Courtesy of the Metropolitan Museum of Art

FIG. 56.   WHITE PORCELAIN SNUFF BOTTLE
IN OPEN WORK DESIGN
Modern.   Red glass stopper.
Courtesy of the Metropolitan Museum of Art

FIG. 57.   SNUFF BOTTLE
Twin.   Porcelain.   Decorated with famille
rose enamel.   Chien Lung period.
1736-1795.
Courtesy of the Metropolitan Museum of Art

FIG. 58. LAVENDER AND GREEN SNUFF
BOTTLE
Jadeite.   Chien Lung.   1736-1795.
Courtesy of the Metropolitan Museum of Art

FIG. 59. SNUFF BOX. FIREGILT. OVAL

Chased in diaper pattern. Enamel miniature.
"Fabiola" after Henner. French.

FIG. 60. FIREGILT SNUFF BOX

Round, heavy repoussé at sides. Miniature
on ivory. Signed Hermandez. French.

FIG. 61. FIREGILT SNUFF BOX

Chased with diaper pattern. Painting on ivory.
"Fishing Party." Signed A. de St. Marc. French.

FIG. 62. IVORY SNUFF BOX

Round. Miniature on ivory set in gold.
French.

FIG. 63. ECCLESIASTICAL ROUND BOX-WOOD
SNUFF BOX

Beautifully carved. Screw top with inner
metal clasp. "Christus."

FIG. 64. REVERSE SIDE, "MARY."

FIG. 65. PAPIER-MÂCHÉ SNUFF BOX

Black with cameo insert of
Pope Pius IX. 1870.

FIG. 66. DARK WOOD SNUFF BOX

Silver ends. Silver Monstrance on
ivory cover. Clasp in silver.
Marked, "Victoria B. F." Italian.

FIG. 67. COPPER SNUFF BOX
Verni Martin. Oval. Painting after "Boucher."

FIG. 68. DARK TORTOISE SHELL SNUFF BOX
Fluted. Gold hinges and gold stars inset.

FIG. 69. SNUFF BOXES MADE OF INDIAN BETEL NUT

Dark brown. Deeply carved on both sides. One with
figures, the other with symbols and flowers.

FIG. 70a. DARK BLUE COMPOSITION SNUFF BOX. Gilt bronze portrait of Voltaire.
FIG. 70b. WOOD SNUFF BOX. Medallion in silver. "Ceres." FIG. 70c. WOOD
SNUFF BOX. General Washington. Medallion in gold. Under glass. Circa 1778.
FIG. 70d. MOTTLED WOOD SNUFF BOX. Medallion in copper of Luther, Churf and
Melanchthon. Dated 1830. Memorial. FIG. 70e. Napoleon and Louise.

FIG. 71. TIN SNUFF BOX
Verni Martin finish. Richly colored. Ballet dancer.

FIG. 72. PEWTER SNUFF BOX
Motto, "Sic Publico Commoda Stabunt."

FIG. 73. BRASS AND BRONZE SNUFF BOX
"England expects every man to do his duty."
Admiral Nelson. Trafalgar. Oct. XXI, MDCCCV.

FIG. 74. APPLE WOOD SNUFF BOX

With five lids. Dog in mother of pearl on bright red ground.

LE FRUIT DEFENDU

FIG. 75. BLACK BONE SNUFF BOX

Adam and Eve. The tree and the serpent.
"Le fruit defendu."

FIG. 76. OVAL BRASS SNUFF BOX

With silver lid and hinge bottom. Floral engraving. "Chiolerie Cio Francisco." 1856.

FIG. 77. BRONZE OCTAGONAL SNUFF BOX.

Head of Gustavus Adolphus. Bottom, coat of arms.

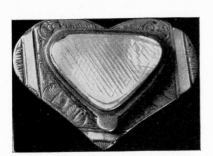

FIG. 78. BRASS AND MOTHER OF PEARL HEART SHAPED SNUFF BOX

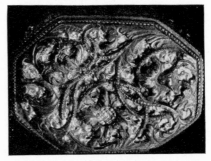

FIG. 79. WROUGHT IRON SNUFF BOX

Very rare. Finely done in vines and flowers. Gold background. Given by a German Prince to Bishop ———— of Washington, D. C.

FIG. 80. EARLY 19TH CENTURY TIN
SNUFF BOX

Said to be portrait of Jenny Lind.
Fashion of 1830.

FIG. 81. TORTOISE SHELL SNUFF BOX

Portrait on ivory Louis XVIII with decoration.
French.

FIG. 82. TORTOISE SHELL BOX WITH GILT
BANDS

Miniature in ivory. Gentleman with
stock. Early 19th century.

FIG. 83. MOTTLED TORTOISE SHELL SNUFF
BOX

Miniature on ivory. Young student.
Light blue background. Gold band.

FIG. 84. PAPIER-MÂCHÉ SNUFF BOX
Copy Romney's portrait of "Cowper."

FIG. 85.   PAPIER-MÂCHÉ SNUFF BOX
Verni Martin.   Ficture of St. Peter.   Done in rich browns.

FIG. 86.   PAPIER-MÂCHÉ SNUFF BOX
Table box.   Old man with red cap trimmed with fur.   Brown
cloak.

FIG. 87. PAPIER-MÂCHÉ SNUFF BOX
Old bearded man with red cloak. 18th century.

FIG. 88. PAPIER-MÂCHÉ SNUFF BOX
"The Dentist Shop." After Teniers.

FIG. 89. PAPIER-MÂCHÉ SNUFF BOX
Master with pipe. Servant bringing beer.

FIG. 90. PAPIER-MÂCHÉ SNUFF BOX
Gaily painted hunting scene. Lines painted in gold.

FIG. 91*a*. BONE SNUFF BOX.

Two finger opening. Book form.
Hot needle engraving. 1847. Spanish.

FIG. 91*b*. BONE SNUFF BOX

Oval with hot needle engraving; lettering in German.

FIG. 91*c*. HORN SNUFF BOX

Brass bound ends. Top ivory with hot point
drawing of flowers.

FIG. 92. PAPIER-MÂCHÉ SNUFF BOX
King Henry of Navarre in action.

FIG. 93. HEAVY TORTOISE SHELL SNUFF BOX
Bound in silver with silver hinges. Fine example of piqué gold work.

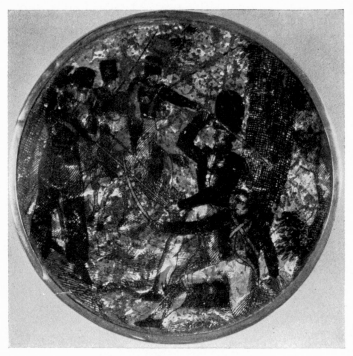

FIG. 94. WOOD SNUFF BOX

Bound in brass. Mosaic top. Made of fish scales in colors.
Soldiers fighting.

FIG. 95. BLONDE TORTOISE SHELL SNUFF BOX

Inlaid with gold. Balloon ascension.
Circa 1783.

FIG. 96. TURQUOISE ENCASED IN SILVER WITH
SILVER TOP AND SPOON

Turquoise insets.

FIG. 97. CHINESE SNUFF BOTTLES

Silver with silver top and spoons. Formerly medicine bottles.

FIG. 98a. DARK TORTOISE SHELL SNUFF BOX
Deeply carved (top). Chinese.

FIG. 98b. SAME. (bottom).

FIG. 99. PORCELAIN SNUFF BOX

Mounted in gold. Profile portrait of Washington. Flanked by sprays of oak leaves. Gilt on a white ground. Germany. (Meissen). 1814-1818.

Courtesy of the Metropolitan Museum of Art

FIG. 100. IVORY AND GOLD SNUFF BOX

Tortoise shell lining. Profile portrait of Franklin in stipple engraving on paper. English. Late 18th or early 19th century.

Courtesy of the Metropolitan Museum of Art

FIG. 101.   TORTOISE SHELL AND GOLD SNUFF
BOX

Portrait of Lafayette painted in grisaille on
a white porcelain plaque.   Probably French.
Late 18th century.

Courtesy of the Metropolitan Museum of Art

FIG. 102.   PAPIER-MÂCHÉ SNUFF BOX

Portrait of "Lady with red bag."   Signed H.
Weber.   1839.

FIG. 103. PAPIER-MÂCHÉ SNUFF BOX
"The Blind Fiddler" after Teniers.

FIG. 104. PAPIER-MÂCHÉ SNUFF BOX
Woman pointing. "Un jour Ernst." "Sobiesky."
French colors down.

FIG. 105.   PAPIER-MÂCHÉ SNUFF BOX
Verni Martin.   Rectangular.   Fine landscape.

FIG. 106.   CLEAR GLASS, PEAR SHAPED
SNUFF BOTTLE

Pewter screw top and tin screw bottom.
Early American.   Circa 1800.

FIG. 107. PAPIER-MÂCHÉ TABLE SNUFF BOX
Painted landscape. Verni Martin finish.

FIG. 108. PAPIER-MÂCHÉ TABLE SNUFF BOX
Painted landscape. Verni Martin finish.

FIG. 109. PAPIER-MÂCHÉ TABLE SNUFF BOX
Painted landscape. Verni Martin finish.

FIG. 110. PAPIER-MÂCHÉ SNUFF BOX
Painted landscape. Verni Martin finish.

FIG. 111. THUNGA WOOD SNUFF BOX LINED WITH
TORTOISE SHELL

Portrait of a lady. French.

FIG. 112. HORN SNUFF BOX, MOUNTED IN GOLD
MINIATURE ON IVORY

Anne, Marchioness of Donegal, by Richard
Cosway. 1765-1770. English.

FIG. 113. SNUFF BOX

On face of box, miniature portrait
Henry VIII. On base, portrait Anne
Boleyn.

Courtesy of the Metropolitan Museum of Art

FIG. 114. TORTOISE SHELL AND BONE SNUFF BOX

Miniature in pen and ink. From collection Grand
Duke Constantinovich. Signed Masins, 1799 (Artist,
Royal Mint, Russia).

FIG. 115. SNUFF BOX

Gold, decorated with panels of opalescent enamels, semé with red
stars, carved and enameled borders. Plaque of purple glass set
with diamond cipher Catherine the Great.

FIG. 116. SNUFF BOX.

Carved gold, encrusted with floral design in enamel. On cover,
portrait of Queen Anne. Gold and enamel.

FIG. 117. POLYCHROME WITH PANELS DEPICTING NAVAL BATTLES AND
SEASCAPES, GOLD-ENAMEL

Courtesy of the Metropolitan Museum of Art

Finis. "Professor Emeritus"